Michelene Wandor

Look Back in Gender

MICHELENE WANDOR is a poet, playwright and critic. From 1971–82 she was Poetry Editor and regularly reviewed plays for *Time Out* magazine. A volume of her stage plays *Five Plays* was published by Playbooks/Journeyman in 1984 and her prolific work for radio includes dramatisations of Dostoyevsky's *The Brothers Karamazov* and a three-part serial of Jane Austen's *Persuasion*. She has published two books of poetry *Upbeat* and *Gardens of Eden* (Journeyman) and a collection of short stories *Guests in the Body* (Virago). As an editor, she has compiled a collection of essays *On Gender and Writing* (Pandora) and four volumes of *Plays by Women* (Methuen). Her book on theatre and sexual politics, *Carry On, Understudies* is published by Routledge.

D0970723

The photograph on the front cover shows Mary Ure as Alison in Osborne's 'Look Back in Anger' (Houston Rogers).

Look Back in Gender

Sexuality and the Family in post-war British drama

Michelene Wandor

Methuen. London and New York

First published in Great Britain in 1987
in simultaneous hardback and paperback editions
by Methuen London Ltd
11 New Fetter Lane, London EC4P 4EE
and in the United States of America
by Methuen Inc, 29 West 35th Street,
New York, NY 10001.
Copyright © 1987 by Michelene Wandor

Acknowledgements
We are grateful to Kathleen Tynan for permission
to reproduce 'The Royal Smut-Hound' by Kenneth Tynan,
and to Celia Mitchell for her assistance.

Printed in Great Britain
by Richard Clay Ltd, Bungay, Suffolk

British Library Cataloguing in Publication Data

Wandor, Michelene
    Look back in gender : sexuality and the
    family in post-war British drama.
    1. Sex in literature   2. English drama—
    20th century—History and criticism
    I. Title
    822'.914'09353   PR739.S4

    ISBN 0–413–56730–3

Contents

v

Contents

Contents

The sound of the trumpets died away and Orlando stood stark naked. No human being, since the world began, has ever looked more ravishing. His form combined in one the strength of a man and a woman's grace.

. . .

Orlando had become a woman – there is no denying it. But in every other respect, Orlando remained precisely as he had been. The change of sex, though it altered their future, did nothing whatever to alter their identity. Their faces remained, as their portraits prove, practically the same. . . Many people . . . holding that such a change of sex is against nature, have been at great pains to prove 1) that Orlando had always been a woman, 2) that Orlando is at this moment a man.

(*Orlando* by Virginia Woolf; 1928)

Introduction

Imagine . . . The imperative of gender

Imagine that Hamlet is a woman. I don't mean imagine an actress playing the character of Hamlet in the play by Shakespeare, and adequately filling both breeches and the character's tragic emotional range, à la Sarah Bernhardt. I mean, imagine the actual play by Shakespeare called *Hamlet*, in which the title role is specifically designated for a female character. The play's title changes to *Hamlette, Princess of Denmark*. Let us investigate the new meanings produced by this gender transformation of the central character.

In Act I, Scene I, the ghost of Hamlette's father appears with something important to communicate. In this opening expositional scene the change of sex necessitates no more than changing the pronouns which refer to the heroine at the end of the scene from 'him' to 'her'. In Act I, Scene II, Hamlette is asked by her mother and uncle/stepfather not to return to her studies in Wittenberg. Hamlette is in anguish at the way her mother has betrayed her dead father by marrying again so quickly. The change in gender here also seems relatively unproblematic – except perhaps that a line such as 'Frailty, thy name is woman' is bound to carry a different and possibly more bitter reverberation if spoken by a woman about her own sex than if spoken by a man about the opposite sex.

However, when Hamlette meets her fellow students Marcellus and Horatio, very important questions are raised about historical accuracy in relation to the period in which the play is set. At that time, only men would have been given access to the kind of student education from which Marcellus and Horatio benefit. In addition, this student friendship, loyalty and comradeship between Horatio and Hamlette, is absolutely central to the play and to Hamlette's sense of her own identity. We thus have to ask why it is that this woman is allowed to be an exception and partake in education on the same terms as men. Is the play deliberately departing from historic convention? Is there some reason why it should go against historical gender expectations? What will be the impact of presenting a heroine who, in the context of Elizabethan tragic drama, will experience emotions and dilemmas which would otherwise only be familiar through the stage world of male heroes?

In Act I, Scene III, the question about gender becomes more complexly sexual. Laertes and Ophelia discuss Hamlet and his apparently fickle affections for Ophelia. When Hamlet is male, the word 'love' means heterosexual love with marriage as a possible goal. If, however, the main character is female, then clearly the meaning of this relationship and the emotional exchange will be different. Either the word 'love' refers merely to an intense friendship between two women (Ophelia and Hamlette) or the relationship is sexual as in the original but with quite different and possibly subversive homosexual implications.

The gender transformation adds a political dimension in Act I, Scene IV when the ghost urges Hamlette to avenge the foul murder of her father. Here, unusually, a woman is being entrusted with the honourable task of setting a disordered state to rights. The spectacle of a woman being asked to purge the state of corruption is likely to produce a tragic heroine of a very different order from, say, a figure such as Antigone. Antigone's function as a tragic heroine is far more passive in her defiance of the state. At no point in her life does Antigone seek to take political power. Her actions are in defence of personal honour, as she seeks to counter an act of injustice against her brother. Antigone represents a critical moral dilemma of conscience, but our newly gendered Hamlette represents both a moral and a political dilemma. Her task is not simply to come to terms with the personal morality of her mother's actions in marrying her uncle, but also to undergo the intellectual anguish of someone who is being forced into a political arena.

The nature of the dilemmas, the motivations and the relationships all take on different aspects according to whether the central character is male or female, and one could go through the entire play plotting each point at which the meaning of any given moment alters along the lines of some of the suggestions made so far. In some ways, *Hamlet* is a particularly suitable play to use in such an exercise because of the nature of the original central character and the dilemmas with which Shakespeare has presented him. It is no coincidence that so many famous actresses have chosen to play the character of Hamlet (as a man) since the anguish he undergoes represents the sensitive, more emotional and introverted side of what is seen to be a 'man's' nature and therefore he has an emotional range which is more accessible to actresses used to portraying emotions that are normally thought to be the province of women. Hamlet is no swashbuckling hero, but a sensitive intellectual, and yet everything about him in the original play is defined by the imperatives of his male gender. His anguish is poignant and gripping precisely because he is being asked to take on the tasks that a 'real man' would take on without question. His refusal to fight and kill can be seen as a matter of honourable conscience-questioning which ends with him fulfilling the role he is expected to play in his final duel. However, if he becomes Hamlette, the ambivalence about fighting could spring from the fact that she is a woman and not used to fighting, so that when she takes part in the final duel she would be subverting the role that is expected of her as a woman.

If we have Hamlet and Hamlette, we have two plays, since the gender of the chief character casts a different set of lights on many of the structural meanings of the play. Questions about historical accuracy, the characters' familial, political and sexual relationships all change and in the process new and different insights are revealed about the meaning and interpretation of the function of gender in the original text.

The gender of a character defines not only his or her biological sexual characteristics, but also implies imaginative and social assumptions about her/his personality, power and place in the world. The exercise with Shakespeare's play, through demonstrating how a change in gender can precipitate other changes in meaning, directs us back to asking new questions about the playwright's original choice of gender. These choices, conscious or unconscious on the playwright's behalf, are as fundamental to the nature of a play's meaning as a playwright's choice of geographical location, historical period, the class and race of characters. Gender is one of the fundamental imperatives in the imaginative creation of the world on stage.

The imperative of gender is something which has scarcely figured at all in the critical analysis and evaluation of plays. And yet the function of gender has been of vital importance since the very beginnings of theatre. The exclusion of women as performers from religious drama, from Greek drama and from the western stage until relatively recently has not been accidental. Women were excluded from the stage because it was not thought proper for them to appear in such a position in public. When female characters were included in plays, they were played by men. And even though there were some exceptions (prehistoric ritual drama, for example, which was conducted by women, or the very much later Commedia dell'arte companies), the received tradition of the theatre presents us with an imaginative world created and controlled by men. In the texts that have come down to us, this is a world of great imaginative power and it is this power in its complex manifestations which informs our approach to the theatre of our own time.

The position of women has changed a great deal in Britain since the latter part of the seventeenth century when women were first allowed to perform on public stages and began to make their mark as playwrights. Feminist movements since the nineteenth century have challenged the traditionally subordinate roles of women in both society and in the theatre, and in the most recent wave of feminism since 1969–70 and the development of the theatrical 'fringe' in the context of British subsidised theatre, many more challenges have been made to traditional male dominance in the theatre. I wouldn't claim that these challenges have altered the face of theatre across the board, but many of the questions asked by feminism about women's place in culture can enable us to throw new and important light on plays written in the past – seen from the point of view of a new and vital analysis of the function of gender in these plays.

In this context, the function of gender means not just looking at female characters but at male characters too. This can only work if it demonstrates the critical ways in which maleness as well as female-ness work in the operation of the theatrical dynamic.

The purpose of this book is fundamentally practical. It seeks to bring new insights to theatre practitioners in the hope that approaches to the production of any of these plays may be illumin-ated. It seeks also to add insights to the work of students studying drama in both a practical and an academic context. My intention is to show that approaching drama from the point of view of the function of gender can expand horizons of meaning, aesthetic pleasure, and the interpretive possibilities of plays, and in some cases enable us to arrive at a much more accurate understanding of exactly how it is that a particular play works so effectively.

Introduction

The book spans the period of post-war British drama from 1956 to the early 1980s. This quarter of a century has seen an extraordinary development in British theatre, from the post-war challenge to West End drawing-room drama, to the politically highly self-conscious work of many playwrights in the 1970s. My concern has been to take many of the critiques and insights developed by feminism and which I have included in my own critical work on the theatre,* and to expand and apply these ideas to the work of individual playwrights, male and female, who constitute the landscape of British radical 'high art' theatre. It is a new mapping of what is, to some extent, a familiar landscape.

Almost all the plays taken from between 1956 and 1968 are plays which are established and influential successes all over the world. They represent peaks of theatrical achievement and in their success show how imaginative work can travel the trajectory from so-called minority art success to massive popular accessibility. Many of these plays are on examination syllabuses, regularly produced by repertory theatres all over the country and have been filmed. Whatever the complex of reasons which made these plays successful and popular, nevertheless they offer a most fruitful field for re-evaluation from the point of view of the function of gender.

The first section of the book looks at plays written while theatrical censorship was still in operation. The second part of the book evaluates plays written since 1968, after censorship was abolished. Because we are still close to the latter period, it is impossible to know for sure which will be the genuinely enduring plays of this period, but I have chosen mainly significant plays, which have attained some measure of public success, in order to see how the function of gender has changed during this period of twenty-five years. In both sections of the book I have included a small number of plays which didn't succeed commercially. I have done this because in analysing other plays some new questions have come up which I have thought could be interestingly illuminated by discussing a less well-known play. In some cases it has been these works which pinpoint some concerns more clearly.

Most of the playwrights discussed in this book are men. Women playwrights are still in the minority, even after the feminist activism of the last fifteen years.† It is very important indeed to understand

---

* See my *Carry On, Understudies*, theatre and sexual politics (Routledge, 1986)
† *Plays by Women*, vols 1, 2, 3 and 4, ed. Michelene Wandor (Methuen)

that men and women write in the same society with the same sets of constraints which sometimes affect them in different ways because of their differential genders. I do not claim, and never would, that men and women write in two separate imaginative spheres. That is a dualistic approach which negates and forecloses discussion, and I am more concerned to open up and illuminate the complex ways in which the gendered imagination works. Of course it is true that a playwright is always influenced by his or her gender, consciously and/or unconsciously, but there are many other important factors too: class, race, social location and the individual's history combine differently through the refracting process of fictional creation. I will, where relevant, be making some comparisons with the different ways in which male and female playwrights have interpreted themes of social interest or produced similar stage imagery.

One of the themes which runs through the book is the way representations of the family and sexuality have developed. There are also changes in conventions of theatrical setting – the relationship between the 'domestic' and the 'public' play, and the relationship of women to politics. Given that this book covers censorship and post-censorship, pre-subsidised theatre and subsidised theatre, pre-political theatre and political theatre, it is not surprising that both content and form should have undergone transformation, and I will chart patterns of change as well as patterns of consistency.

This book is a continuation of my work in *Carry on, Understudies*, which documented and discussed the ways in which feminism and sexual politics influenced and helped produce a new kind of theatre movement in the 1970s. This book takes up many of the same themes, but applies them to the work of individual playwrights. Themes such as the relationship between the personal and the political, the public and the private, domestic/historical/epic drama, the relationship between personal violence and political violence, the ways in which playwrights struggled to represent or suppress sexual relationships, the representation of family relationships and the recurring image of the mother figure, are all themes which will be discussed with direct reference to the function of gender.

A final personal note. My involvement in theatre has been continuous over the past thirty years. At first as enthusiastic theatre-goer, then as actress, then as critic and playwright. For me, as for many other people, a sense of what theatre could achieve began in the mid-1950s and continued through the exciting social artistic and political changes after 1968. In the early 1980s the landscape is changing again and once more we are at a crossroads. It is a moment which is far less clear than either 1956 or 1968 were, and perhaps it is for this reason that we need to look back at these two critical recent periods in theatrical history, for the future of theatre will come from the impetus for change given to it both by those who are politically vociferous, and also by those who do not consider themselves 'political', but absorb influences from their world and refract them through their individual imaginations.

Part One

After the War was Over . . .

A Labour government came into power at the end of World War Two, followed by the establishment of the Welfare State, the National Health Service, and secondary education which was for the first time free to everyone. These changes, plus many others, directly and fundamentally affected the changing social roles of men and women, and the function of the family.

The concept of the family involved both parents: men returning from the war to build a new peacetime life as well as the women who were returning to the home to take up their conventional role as wives and mothers. Recent feminist social critiques have shown the ways in which emerging sociology, psychological theories, social policy and women's magazines tried to return women to contented roles in the family after their involvement in the war economy.* After such a long period at war, with the entire population geared towards the war economy, with matters of survival, death, injury, hardship, regular accompaniments to daily life, and the absence of a large part of the country's male population, this transition to a peacetime that was producing a new and more affluent world to live in was bound to be exciting, traumatic and to alter many of the landmarks of pre-war thinking and imagining. Adjustments were on the agenda for men as well as for women, and in the popular press it was seen as important to help men adjust to a domestic life of family and breadwinnerdom, while women adjusted to their new lives on the assumption that the man would now be the chief and ever-present breadwinner.

This attempt to rationalise familial roles for men and women did not always take full account of all the realities – such as the fact that large numbers of women continued to do paid work well into the 1950s, many of them in effect doing two jobs, at home and at work. The point is that new emphasis was put on the family as the cornerstone of social reconstruction. New housing was being built, the Education and Welfare State, and a Health Service promising

* See *Women and the Welfare State*, Elizabeth Wilson, Tavistock Publications.

better health for the children of the new families, producing new attitudes to class and sex. Certainly these material improvements in the conditions of people's lives broadened people's aspirations, giving rise to a Utopian possibility that the class and sex wars were over now that everyone had the same opportunities.

The 1950s was a decade in which many changes took place rapidly; the rebuilding of an entire society from a war economy to a relative affluence, and the beginnings of a new youth-directed culture; American films, rock and roll, and a mass consumerism began to match the earning power and expectations of young people. All this was the backdrop to a much higher and more explicit profile for sexuality:

> . . . by the fifties sexual potency in men and sexual responsiveness in women began to be seen as explicitly desirable qualities, emphasised . . . in such opinion moulders as the problem pages of women's magazines.
>
> Elizabeth Wilson (*Women and the Welfare State*, p. 66)

In America, *Playboy* magazine, with its pneumatic female pin-ups, created a new image for the virile male. What is very interesting indeed about this period is that ideas of great importance were being conveyed to men which involved a fundamental change of image for them. To that of the military hero so prevalent during the war (and afterwards; in Britain two years of military National Service continued to be compulsory for men until the late 1950s), a new image was added of the new breadwinner male, the head of the family, a man who expected access to a fulfilled sexuality in reality, and a glamorous sexuality in fantasy life.

Inevitably with this more public profile for heroic and feminine sexuality and new images in the media, particularly in films, there were changes in the attitudes of ordinary people and of the state to familial and personal mores. Through the Fifties, divorce and sexual reform began to be matters that were widely debated:

> The 1950s and 1960s witnesses the cumulative removal of customary and legal restraints on certain forms of sexual behaviour, and upon their public portrayal in print or by the visual arts or for commercial purposes. Legal restrictions on the freedom of married people to escape from the bonds which used to be defended as essential safeguards for the integrity of monogamous marriage have been relaxed, and the sexual freedom of men and women has been enlarged.
>
> (Finer Report, Vol. 1, 1974: 7)

During the late 1960s a number of liberal legal reforms went through Parliament, relaxing restrictions on divorce, contraception and abortion, and with limited reforms for homosexuality.

In the Arts this liberalisation was evident in the debate about censorship. The censorship of books was tested in a number of cases: the best-known of these being the case of *Lady Chatterley's Lover* by D.H. Lawrence, in 1960. Theatre censorship was finally abolished in 1968. Where books or films could be challenged by censorship post-publication, theatre censorship had been applied by the Lord Chamberlain before a play could be produced, and this inevitably meant before a play was published. It is probably difficult for anyone who has grown up with the theatre since 1968 to imagine what living with official censorship was like; it must have had a series of interesting, frustrating and contradictory effects on the imaginations of playwrights. Playwrights could not write without some awareness that certain kinds of subject matter and forms of expression would be taboo, knowing that if they did take risks they were likely at some point to come up against censorship or theatres who might be reluctant to do plays that would cause problems.

The brief on the basis of which censorship operated was vague, to say the least. Under the Theatres Act of 1843, the Lord Chamberlain operated pre-production censorship, and his approval was essential before any play could receive a public production. The guidelines were never really very clear, despite an attempt by a committee in 1909 to suggest some:

> The committee said that the Lord Chamberlain should be able to refuse a licence only if a play submitted might reasonably be held: [a] to be indecent; [b] to contain offensive personalities; [c] to represent on the stage in an invidious manner a living person or any person recently dead; [d] to do violence to the sentiment of religious reverence; [e] to be calculated to conduce to crime or violence; [f] to be calculated to impair friendly relations with any foreign power; [g] to be calculated to cause a breach of the peace.
> (Terry Browne, *Playwrights Theatre*, Pitman, 1975, p. 56)

Such vagueness and ambiguity lent itself to the entirely unilateral situation that what was considered indecent and offensive was that which was likely to offend the Lord Chamberlain – see p. 73 for Kenneth Tynan's brilliant analysis of the precise codes which operated behind censorship.

Until 1968, anything that referred to homosexuality had to be cut, there were heavy restrictions on the use of 'bad language', a lot of watchdogging on forms of dress, physical behaviour or any gesture which hinted too overtly at any kind of active heterosexuality. The representation of sexuality in any explicit sense was thus being seriously repressed in the imaginations of writers of the 1950s and 1960s who took any kind of radical perspective on society. They had to find solutions as to how to represent sexuality in their dialogue and stage action, and often did so in imaginatively exciting ways, as well as in indirect and oblique forms. Meanwhile, another part of the State was actually conceding to demands for a more permissive recognition of the possibilities of both heterosexual and homosexual choice, options within marriage, and the move to separate sexual pleasure from reproduction for women as well as for men, in order to make it easier for individuals to exercise wider personal, moral and sexual choices.

It is the tension between the social advances in the 1950s and 1960s with regard to sexual mores, and the theatrical repression which makes the plays of the period particularly interesting. In addition, the contrast between wartime and peacetime domesticity put new strains on the family. The war economy produced an ideology where men and women were united in their national efforts even though they had different gender roles, but in some ways war also broke down certain aspects of gender roles. Men in the army, for example, had to look after themselves, and although this is not a common image of heroic depictions of war, it is actually very important for the way in which men developed their own self image, learning by necessity how to darn socks, cook, wash clothes and perform the kinds of jobs that under peacetime conditions would be done by women. And at the same time, because men were off in the army, women at home had to take on not just responsibilities as heads of their families, but also many of the activities and functions that men would have performed during peacetime. After the war, there was, in theory, a re-jigging of public and private roles back to the way they had been before, and this produced an interesting tension and gender contradiction which had its effect on the way the next generation began to perceive the world.

Matters of national and social identity, the notion of heroism, and the nature of class also have their bearing on the function of gender, as does the role of the family and the way sexuality in its broadest possible sense is represented. It is appropriate, therefore, to begin with the play in which all these questions came together with a new and radical force – *Look Back in Anger* by John Osborne.

Heroism, Crises of Manhood and the Kitchen Sink

Look Back in Anger and
A Patriot For Me by John Osborne

John Osborne's *Look Back in Anger* is a compelling and powerful play which helped initiate a new way of showing contemporary life in the theatre. In it gender functions centrally in the way the play is structured and conveys its social and sexual messages.

Stage directions tended to be fulsome in the social realist plays of the 1950s, crucial to establishing their social setting: *Look Back in Anger* is set in the Porters' one-room flat in a large Midlands town. The one-room flat is significant, not just because it tells us that they can't afford to live anywhere larger, but because it brings together in a real and symbolic way all the different living functions that the conventional family abode would have: the cluster of kitchen, eating, entertaining and sleeping areas suggests a hothouse of interpersonal relations. The school of theatre which this play helped to generate became known as 'kitchen-sink theatre', an ironic misnomer if ever there was one, since while the kitchen sink may sometimes have been on stage, it was very rarely the experience of the woman who would normally be at the kitchen sink which was the focus of the play. The sink itself, or any other kind of stage apparatus which represented the sink, functions more as an emblem of the male psyche in crisis.

The opening 'domestic' scene shows us Jimmy and Cliff – a kind of double act – reading the Sunday newspapers in comradely chaos. By contrast, Alison, Jimmy's wife, is standing ironing. The stage directions say that she is ironing one of Jimmy's shirts and wearing another. Thus she is servicing the domestic scene and demonstrating to the audience in an immediate visual way that she is Jimmy's property. In visual terms she may dominate the action by standing, but the emotional attention is on Jimmy.

Jimmy is one of the generation who faced compulsory National

8

Service, and he is obsessed by the past of the upper class. From the first, he is full of verbal energy, goading Alison:

> I think I can understand how her Daddy must have felt when he came back from India . . . The old Edwardian brigade do make their brief little world look pretty tempting. All home-made cakes and croquet, bright ideas, bright uniforms . . . What a romantic picture. Phoney, too, of course.

Jimmy and Alison have been married for three years and she tells Cliff that they hadn't slept together before marriage:

> . . . And, afterwards, he actually taunted me with my virginity. He was quite angry about it, as if I had deceived him in some strange way. He seemed to think an untouched woman would defile him.

Sexuality, overt and covert, are the stuff of the exchanges, not just between Jimmy and Alison but also between Alison and Cliff. Throughout the play it is interesting that the only apparently unfraught physical contact between characters (until the very end) is that between Jimmy and Cliff, who every so often rough-house together in an innocent, covertly homo-erotic way, and also between Cliff and Alison. Cliff is physical, cuddly and affectionate with Alison in a brotherly way and the contact between them is not sexual. By contrast, the contact between Alison and Jimmy is always fraught, sometimes violent, even when it may be playful. Although Jimmy describes Cliff as 'a sexy little Welshman' there is no evidence that Cliff has any sexual relationship of any kind with anyone at all, male or female. He is just there, asexual, necessary as a foil for the two sexual protagonists. At one point in this first scene, Jimmy and Cliff fight, and bump into Alison who burns her arm on the iron; her physical pain is an emblem of the psychological and emotional pain which Jimmy causes Alison, in which Cliff symbolically colludes.

Alison represents all that Jimmy despises in a ruling class which no longer conveys an old-style patriotism. But she is constantly attacked on the basis of her femaleness; she may be superior on the basis of her class, but Jimmy conveys the superiority of his gender, though this is never enough for him. The gender conflict is a battleground:

> Have you ever noticed how noisy women are? . . . The way they kick the floor about simply walking over it? Or have you watched them sitting at their dressing tables, dropping their weapons and banging down their bits of boxes and brushes and lipsticks?

When Jimmy and Alison are finally alone, there is an awkward admission from Jimmy: 'There's hardly a moment when I'm not – watching or wanting you. I've got to hit out somehow.' This encapsulates the way sexual desire and violence are scarcely differentiated from one another in Jimmy's psyche – a very tortured state of mind for a young man. Jimmy's search for a cause and his sadness that there is no more patriotism left, or at any rate no patriotism which he can be part of, leads him to give a nod of almost envy towards homosexuals:

> Sometimes I almost envy old Gide and the Greek Chorus boys. Oh, I'm not saying that it mustn't be hell for them a lot of the time. But at least they do seem to have a cause – not a particularly good one, it's true. But plenty of them do seem to have a revolutionary fire about them, which is more than you can say for the rest of us.

During this first Act, sexuality is very much on the agenda of the play both in its text and in its sub-text. The climax of Act One is Jimmy's speech about Alison's sexuality and reproductive potential which, given that we know she is pregnant (she has told Cliff but not yet told Jimmy) carries a brutal irony:

> If only something – something would happen to you to wake you out of your beauty sleep! (*Coming in close to her.*) If you could have a child and it would die. Let it grow, let a recognisable human face emerge from that little mass of indiarubber and wrinkles. (*She retreats away from him.*) Please, if only I could watch you face that. I wonder if you might become a recognisable human being yourself. But I doubt it. (*She moves away stunned and leans on the gas stove, down left. He stands rather helplessly on his own.*) Do you know, I have never known the great pleasure of lovemaking when I didn't desire it myself. Oh, it's not that she hasn't her own kind of passion. She has the passion of a python. She just devours me whole every time as if I were some over-large rabbit. That's me. That bulge round her navel – if you're wondering what it is – it's me. Me, buried alive down there and going mad, smothered in that peaceful looking coil. Not a sound, not a flicker from her – she doesn't even rumble a little. You'd think that this indigestible mess would stir up some kind of tremor in those distended overfed tripes – but not her!

Sexuality and motherhood are part of the same nexus of associations with femaleness for Jimmy. In order to attack Alison, he has to attack her not just as a female sexual being but as a potential mother, and paradoxically – and powerfully – he attacks her as some kind of inadequate distorted mother of himself. It is as if he is accusing Alison of not allowing him to give birth to his own self. In

10

revenge he resorts to words, to a literal voice, while Alison's silence is seen as yet another weapon and a threat to his own voice. Whether or not his verbal potency stands as compensation for sexual insecurity, it is clearly presented in opposition to the one thing Alison has which Jimmy can't have: her potential for mother-hood. He may have the power of words, but she has the silent power to give birth. The 'python' metaphor encapsulates Jimmy's fear of female sexual and maternal power. Throughout this first Act, the domestic territory is silently maintained by Alison, while it is given active life by Jimmy's words and on Jimmy's terms.

In Act Two Alison is again doing domestic chores, the men at leisure. There are some illuminating stage directions about Helena, Alison's friend:

> Her sense of matriarchal authority makes most men who meet her anxious, not only to please but to impress, as if she were the gracious representative of visiting royalty. In this case, the royalty of that middle class womanhood, which is so eminently secure in its divine right, that it can afford to tolerate the parliament, and reasonably free assembly of its menfolk.

Again, the class critique is displaced on to the sexual critique. There is a scene between the two women in which they are relaxed and friendly, but the bulk of their conversation is about the men, rather than themselves. Alison describes the first months of her marriage in a different kind of ménage à trois with Hugh, a childhood friend of Jimmy's:

> I felt as though I'd been dropped in a jungle . . . Together they were frightening. They both came to regard me as a sort of hostage from those sections of society they had declared war on.

Jimmy is a rebel in class terms, but in terms of the world of this play, the only way in which he can construct a battleground that has any meaning for him is if the opposition is female. It would have been possible for the playwright to choose a man to embody the class conflict about which Jimmy is supposed to feel so strongly. The fact that a woman has been chosen is significant and indicates that the play's primary concern is not class but a turmoil in Jimmy's mind about the nature of his masculine identity, in which class is a secondary component. Alison describes Jimmy:

> He'd come to the party on a bicycle, he told me, and there was oil all over his dinner jacket. It had been such a lovely day, and he'd been in the sun. Everything about him seemed to burn, his face, the

edges of his hair glistened and seemed to spring off his head, and his eyes were so blue and full of the sun . . . Jimmy went into battle with his axe swinging round his head – frail, and so full of fire. I had never seen anything like it. The old story of the knight in shining armour – except that his armour didn't really shine very much.

It is Jimmy's inability to identify a social cause for his 'heroic' passions which leads him to put all his energy into the domestic war – to the point where he claims as his the emotions which might normally be thought Alison's prerogative:

> I knew more about love . . . betrayal and death when I was ten years old than you will probably ever know in all your life.

In this familial battleground, Cliff takes on an interesting role. He is someone with whom both Alison and Jimmy can be friendly, but only because he is no sexual threat to either. Friendship and sexuality are shown to be mutually exclusive. He is also a substitute – an adult stand-in – for the child they do not have; procreation and motherhood are seen as problematic in this oddball family. Both Jimmy and Alison's mothers are 'bad' – Jimmy's because she didn't care about him, Alison's because she is such an upper-class cow. However, there is one good mother in the play – Hugh's mother, who put up the money to help Jimmy set up the sweet stall on which he works.

Act Three is a mirror image of Act One, except that this time Helena, who has replaced Alison, is ironing. Jimmy has now transferred his one-man private music-hall act into goading Helena, with Cliff still his willing stooge. There is a moment when Jimmy admits to Cliff: 'You're worth half a dozen Helenas to me or to anyone.' Jimmy anguishes on the desperate way in which men are supposed both to need and hate women, and at this point the now famous quote occurs:

> I suppose people of our generation aren't able to die for good causes any longer. We had all that done for us, in the thirties and the forties, when we were still kids . . . There aren't any good brave causes left. If the big bang does come and we all get killed off, it won't be in aid of the old-fashioned, grand design. It'll just be for the Brave New-nothing-very-much-thank-you. About as pointless and inglorious as stepping in front of a bus. No, there's nothing left for it, me boy, but to let yourself be butchered by the women.

Nostalgia for a former nationalistic heroism, and the threat of the nuclear bomb, leave only a cynical decision to be psychically killed by the women: as if women were as dangerous as the enemy in war and the 'big bang'.

When Alison returns, she and Helena again have a scene together, with a conversation against the backdrop of Jimmy playing jazz trumpet as he did in the first scene between them. It is as if the women's voices are not to be allowed to have stage space of their own, but Jimmy's voice, in this case through the trumpet rather than his actual verbal voice, must always be there to remind us of him. We learn here that Alison has lost the baby that she was carrying, and Jimmy shrugs off the loss of this child because, he says, it isn't his first loss. Helena leaves, refusing to take part in the kind of suffering that Jimmy dictates. The last thing he gives Helena as she leaves his flat, is a dress. As long as the women in the play are wearing his shirts, they stand some chance of being born into a form of being over which he has control. By handing Helena a dress, Jimmy indicates that her femaleness is defined by her and not by him.

Alison finally capitulates to Jimmy on his terms. She has lost her child and the ability, perhaps, to have other children. Jimmy has had to destroy the possibility of motherhood in her, in order to gain her as a 'mother' for himself, and his victory over her class has been achieved in terms of her gender. The two retrace their steps into the playroom of bears and squirrels, a childlike pre-sexual place where they can find some peace and rapport. The play ends with Alison's arms around Jimmy, comforting him, so that any maternal qualities she may have had are from now on to be exclusively for him. It is sad, it is tragic, and it is all at her expense, although one has to allow her the credit of having made the decisions herself. She could have stayed away; Helena was able to refuse Jimmy's demands. But the dynamic of their relationship – and, indeed, that of the play – is predicated upon Jimmy's needs. It is Jimmy's search for a social/class identity, and an individual/male identity which is the central subject matter of the piece. There is no equivalent focus given to Alison. The stage action never follows Alison offstage but remains on Jimmy's territory. Alison is not given either any significant education or an occupation. Helena is at least an actress and one has a sense that she knows her place in the world. Jimmy is a rebel, the stage world is his territory. Alison is also a rebel in terms of her class, but the stage territory is not hers, a paradox, since the domestic is supposed to be female territory. The play is male-centred in its focus, and centring the action upon one gender causes the dynamic of the action, character development and the function of all the characters to radiate outwards from the central male figure.

The need for heroism (male) and sexual identity (male) are the subject matter of the play. Jimmy's anguish is expressed through the secondary castigation of a ruling class which has left him nothing to fight for, and a woman whom he sees as a threat and has to destroy metaphorically. He is at least the boss in his own home – a pyrrhic victory, since it is predicated on misogyny, a profound insecurity about male identity, and an uncertainty about the family as a model for the future. Jimmy's relationship with Alison presents us also with a potent example of one of the most important recurring images in the drama of this period: the love–hate relationship men have with the mother figure, in which emotional dependence, a resentment at such dependence, and a desire to destroy, are all combined.

Osborne's play *A Patriot For Me*, first produced nine years later in 1965, is stylistically very different. Instead of the hothouse domestic focus of the one-room flat we have just seen, *A Patriot* is epic and historical. The scenes are of varied lengths and take place in many different locations; the dialogue is more formal. This play was first produced three years before the end of censorship and the Lord Chamberlain made a number of demands on the original version which would have made nonsense of much of its theme and substance, given that male homosexuality is at its centre.

The style of the play prefigures some of the agitprop plays of the 1970s – perhaps inevitable when a writer is dealing with a taboo subject and wants to convey new information to the audience. There is a short scene in which a doctor, an expert on homosexuality, gives a lecture which obviously has a dramatic place in the play, but is also a device to present information to the audience.

The play is set in eastern Europe in 1890 (perhaps the period of great heroic causes which Alison's Colonel father refers to in *Look Back in Anger*). The central figure is Redl, a bright young officer in the Austro–Hungarian army, a workaholic who keeps to himself, and is earmarked for promotion. Redl is a fine soldier and in the first scene he is a second at a duel in which a friend dies in his arms.

The traditional manly way of settling honour with a duel, by an individual with a cause, is presented in the first scene. Military and personal male values are seen as synonymous:

> A good soldier always knows another one. That's what comradeship is. It's not an empty thing, not an empty thing at all. It's knowing the *value* of other men. And cherishing it.

In military life comradeship is seen as a material and validated reality; here is spelled out in words what we have already implicitly witnessed between Jimmy and Cliff. Redl is seen as 'dignified and strikes everyone as the type of a gentleman and distinguished officer of the Royal and Imperial Army' – the stuff of which successful officers are made.

In Madame Anna's nightclub we see also that Redl is a misogynist. When a waiter remarks that a girl is 'beautiful', he replies, 'Garbage often is'. As he is groomed for promotion, his superiors decide that he needs a socially advantageous marriage, and a Countess is enlisted:

> He's steadfast, sober, industrious, orderly, he likes orderly things, hates chaos. That's why marriage would suit him so well.

The relationship between Redl and the Countess is interesting on both public and private counts. They are lovers, but of a rather opportunistic kind. The Countess is set up to spy on Redl and their relationship at times is closer to that of client and prostitute – for example, Redl never kisses her in bed. The Countess is never given her own stage space – as in *Look Back*, the action is predicated entirely on what happens to the male characters, and so we have little knowledge about her motivation in this relationship beyond the sense of power deriving from the fact that she spies on him, writing regular reports to her employers about his behaviour. She is cynical about men:

> But then, when you think of the men one knows who are married and who they're married *to*, and what their real snotty little longings are underneath their proud watch and chains, their constant broken, sidelong glances.

And she has contempt for military comradeship: 'I'm afraid I simply can't understand the army or why any man is ever in it.'

The conflict that Redl may feel between this heterosexual liaison and his homosexuality is shown by the fact that he has nightmares when he is with the Countess. As in *Look Back*, there is the implication that the sexual influence of a woman is suffocating:

> Do you know: the only time I drink heavily is when I'm with you?
> No, I didn't mean that. But when you're badgering me and sitting on
> my head, and, and, I can't breathe.'

Redl is personally vulnerable, while the Countess is emotionally
impervious.

Redl picks up a young soldier (possibly a decoy) and there is a
short scene with the two men in bed, after which Redl is beaten up
by other young soldiers. This is one of the scenes the censor wanted
to cut. The drag ball scene which opens Act Two was also targeted
by the censor – which would have made complete nonsense of the
entire play, since it is in this scene that we see the ironies and
paradoxes of the military way of life as the emblem of manhood
being confirmed and undermined by the practice of transvestism,
which reveals their subversive homosexuality.

There is a long note by the author, giving careful details about the
different kinds of gay types; it is ironic that such attention is paid to
'women' when men are controlling their representation, in the
sense that the male author is writing them, but also in the indirect
sense that it is the male characters who decide when and how and to
what extent they ape the appearance and behaviour of women.
Women, who are seen as inimical to military camaraderie, are also
the route to a kind of personal liberation. The Baron comments that
the drag ball is 'a celebration of the individual against the rest'. And
another character, Kuntz, comments:

> You see, this is a place for people to come together. People who are
> very often in their everyday lives, rather lonely and even miserable
> and feel hunted.

What is fascinating about the tone of this play from the perspective of today, when plays about homosexuality are not as rare or as
dangerous as they were considered in the second half of the 1960s, is
the way in which there is neither a high moral tone about homosexuality nor any kind of weak apologia. What is presented is an all-male
society which is complete and self-contained and in which the very
strong comradeship between men is extended to the sexual arena.
The conflict between the public macho image of the military and the
private needs of some of the individuals within it, produces a social
and political tension, personified in Redl. His unease with the camp
banter with which so many other characters are at home, sets him

apart from them.

Redl's crime is not that he is a homosexual, since we know that the army tolerates homosexuality as long as it is played by certain rules. The crime is that he doesn't mind if what is suppressed comes to the surface; love letters, presents. Perhaps Redl is not satisfied with the gap between what he appears to be and what he actually is, and he begins to be careless in everything but his job. The military machine, however, will not tolerate public efficiency without private acceptance of its rules of behaviour. This makes Redl dispensable and the scapegoat who is sacrificed to warn others that the rules of private behaviour must be observed.

Throughout, Redl never compromises on the primary values of honour and manhood. He gets very angry when women 'take away' men (usually by marriage), the idea being that women are dangerous because they intervene in male/male relationships. In the dramatic structure of the play, the critical change in Redl's behaviour happens after he has had heterosexual contact with the Countess, as if he has been violated by the outside world, represented here by women.

A Patriot For Me explores the absent centre of *Look Back in Anger*: it confronts the concept of patriotism and a national 'cause' through an army, one of the institutions set up to defend such values. Osborne explores the dynamic of this male-dominated section of society, largely 'free' of the 'threat' of women, with the implication that such a society offers the possibility of a kind of Utopia, since whatever the nationalistic causes the army might be fighting for, the central personal cause (which is of crucial importance to all the military men) is the existence of the army and male camaraderie. Redl's behaviour threatens the security of this world and he therefore becomes a sacrificial martyr.

The trauma and personal worry about the family, male sexuality and heroism so evident in *Look Back*, have been resolved here by presenting the army as both cause and substitute family, a milieu in which men satisfy each other in all the important aspects of human relationships. Here subjective concerns between men are the dominant focus of the dramatic theatrical and character action, with none of the important emotions displaced onto relationships with women, who remain dangerous, not even tempting, outsiders, both in relation to the male characters, and to the structural dynamic of the play.

17

These two plays by John Osborne, which straddle the first period of time under discussion, are fascinating contradictions; demonstrations of entrenched and tortured misogyny as an imaginative by-product of some important trail-blazing. Powerful theatrical craft refracts an emotional honesty about crises for men in the 1950s and 1960s, their fears of female sexuality and motherhood, and their validation of worlds of personal and political power in which the only important relationships are between men. Such validation, including the defiant breach of the taboo on homosexuality, cannot accommodate women as part of its world view.

The Jewish Family, Women and Politics

The Wesker Trilogy

Chicken Soup with Barley was first performed at the Belgrade Theatre in Coventry in 1958. Like Osborne, Wesker presents detailed stage directions about the domestic interior. This time we are in a busy family home with a history, a cosy basement living room with an invisible kitchen. For Wesker the domestic functions are separated not just for dramatic reasons but also because for him the concept of the family, and the place of the woman at its centre, is not as problematic as it is for Osborne – indeed, the Jewish family is central in the trilogy and the links between the generations is as much political as it is personal.

The play is set in 1936 during a period of increasing anti-Semitism in Europe and England, and the spotlight is turned on an East End Jewish family. From the beginning it is clear that Sarah is the dominant character; her husband Harry is described in stage directions as 'the antithesis of Sarah. He is amiable but weak'. Sarah mocks his keenness for books; in her eyes he is a dreamer who refuses to 'communicate'. Communication, emotional and verbal, has a high priority between the members of this family. Here there is no question of searching for causes. Sarah is a political activist, a member of the Communist Party; Dave, her future son-in-law, is joining the International Brigade to fight in Spain. The language is vigorous, full of high emotion. Sarah rushes around, nurturing her family, arguing about politics. She is proud of her fiery daughter Ada and her tough son Ronnie.

During the bustle of the first scene the conversation centres round the fact that they are all about to go off on a demonstration. The keynote of political commitment is presented through Sarah. Her ideals are expressed by contrast with the way she sees Cissy, her sister-in-law:

I hate her! Not a bit of warmth, not a bit . . .! What is the good of

being a socialist if you're not warm? People like that can't teach love
and brotherhood . . . Love comes now. You have to start with love.
How can you talk about socialism otherwise.

There is no epic setting here; political activism is brought into the
home and presented as a powerful source of emotional security, and
of urgent political commitment to causes outside the home. No
distinction is made between them.

Act Two takes place in 1946, with the family now in a block of
flats. Sarah still gets at Harry for not wanting to work; he is as tired,
evasive and shifty as he was ten years before. Sarah goes to work
and also leaves food cooking, maintaining the family both from
within and without. They are all still Communist Party members,
with tremendous energy after the war, but Ada and Dave are
planning to leave London and live in the country. A new definition
of socialism is beginning to emerge in terms of a commitment to a
personal, family-based lifestyle:

> Remember this, Ronnie: the family should be a unit and your work
> and your life should be part of one existence, not something hacked
> about by a bus queue and office hours . . .

Ada and Dave's views anticipate those of the hippy 1960s; Ada
sees industrial progress as the enemy and she appeals for a much
more individualised understanding:

> What right have we to care? How can we care for a world outside
> ourselves when the world inside is in disorder?

– echoing Jimmy Porter's desperate need for personal security
before he can get to grips with the world. Sarah, by contrast,
associates personal security with a strong family. She is afraid the
family will break up; her sense of social vitality can exist only when
she has a strong sense of the family.

It is ironic that the picture of the family to which Sarah cleaves so
passionately is contradicted by the nature of the family of which she
is the centre. She continually harangues Harry for not being able to
carry out the traditional male role of breadwinner. Harry has always
resisted this role; he is a dreamer, he goes to the cinema, he cannot
keep a job. Throughout the play the nature of manhood and the
male role is under stress and open to question. As Ronnie comments: 'I don't suppose there is anything more terrifying to a man
than his own sense of failure.' Harry's passivity becomes physical
and material when he has his first stroke, during Act Two.

Unlike *Look Back*, here the gender roles are reversed and it is Sarah whose voice literally dominates, and it is Harry's silence which symbolises disintegration. He ends up being physically unable to talk, symbolic of his inability to give voice to his concerns. Harry's philosophy, when he *does* manage to express it, is passive and significantly addressed to his son rather than his wife:

> You can't alter people, Ronnie. You can only give them love and hope they will take it.

Act Three takes place ten years later after Harry has had a second stroke and is paralysed and slightly senile. The family which has meant everything to Sarah is changing. Ada has moved away with her husband Dave; they have two children and he makes furniture. Ronnie works as a cook. Harry becomes symbolic of family disintegration: physically frail, unable to control his bowels. Harry becomes a child, and Sarah becomes his mother. When we first meet Sarah she is 37 and it is implied that she is no longer sexually active in her relationship with Harry.

As the action moves into December 1956, we have further evidence of the disintegration of the values and causes which Sarah has taken so much for granted: she has to deal with the rudeness and bureaucracy of the welfare state, and the new flats are lonely. Sarah has some fulfilment in her mother–son relationship with Ronnie. Ronnie questions Sarah about Hungary and attacks her for her optimism, saying she never taught him there could be any political doubts. Ronnie says:

> Why do I feel ashamed to use words like democracy and freedom and brotherhood? They don't have meaning any more.

Whereas Porter regrets the passing of the values of the upper classes, Ronnie Kahn regrets the passing of the old socialist ideals as inadequate to deal with the atom bomb which casts a shadow over the Final Act.

Although Sarah is the custodian of the political and family values, and dominates the domestic territory, when it comes to passing on these values to the next generation, it is Ronnie whom she tries to convince. Ada questions her ideas, and then disappears to become a good wife and mother to Dave. As Sarah becomes more powerful and dominant, and Harry becomes weaker and more physically dependent, there seems to be a need for the mantle of commitment and questioning to be passed to the next male in line – Ronnie.

21

Harry too chooses Ronnie as confidant, with the suggestion of male bonding in the face of an overpowering woman. Ronnie's articulated doubts about socialist values complement Harry's silent protest. Sarah's final concern, while expressed in generalisations which use the male pronoun, brings together political ideals and personal passions again:

> Socialism is my light . . . A way of life. A man *can* be beautiful . . . I've got to have light. I am a simple person, Ronnie, and I've got to have light and love . . .

The values carried by the mother in the family are equated to political values:

> Someone told her socialism was happiness so she joined the Party. . . . The only thing that mattered was to be happy and eat. Anything that made you unhappy or stopped you from eating was the fault of Capitalism . . . the East End was a big mother.

At the end Sarah and Ronnie confront one another, socialist certainty and doubt enacted in a powerful mother–son argument. The personal remains political in spite of the fact that Ronnie attacks Sarah where it hurts most: 'The family you always wanted has disintegrated and the great ideal you always cherished has exploded in front of your eyes. But you won't face it.'

Roots, the second play of the trilogy, first performed in May 1959, is set in Norfolk in a ramshackle house. The play opens with another maternal image – Jenny putting her child to bed. Almost immediately her husband enters with a pain in his back. Some of the motifs present in the previous play are repeated; domestic territory is very much the woman's: as soon as the man enters onto domestic territory, he brings some sense of incapacity, a physical illness.

Jenny's sister Beatie, arrives home for a visit, and they have a ritual family chat about matters that concern their own feelings and lives compared with the scene between Alison and Helena, who talk only about Jimmy. Early in *Roots*, Beatie quotes Ronnie. The continuity with the first play in the trilogy is through Ronnie who does not appear; he is a kind of Godot figure, and, like Godot, imposes his values on the people and the dynamic of the action.

Although the action centres around Beatie and her family on their domestic territory, and is in an immediate sense controlled by the women, there is a subtle alternative gender bias in the conceptual influence of the figure of Ronnie. Beatie becomes a symbolic mother, carrying Ronnie around in her head. Every time she quotes from him she is trying to give birth to him through her voice. He has encouraged her to talk the way his mother talked. He loves words, uses them as 'bridges'. Ronnie appreciates books, paintings, and classical music – follows 'high art' as his father Harry did, carrying values from both parents. He is not interested in popular culture; comics, football or rock and roll. He stands up on chairs when he wants to make speeches, and Beatie imitates him, allowing herself a little moment of irony on the nature of Ronnie's influences:

> Once we're married and I got babies I won't need to be interested in half the things I got to be interested in now.

Much of Beatie's conversation with her family consists of testing out Ronnie's ideas. Beatie quotes Ronnie's views, taken both from his father – 'you can't change people . . . you can only give them some love and hope they'll take it', and from his mother – 'socialism isn't talking all the time, it's living, it's singing, it's dancing, it's being interested in what goes on around you'.

Beatie also talks about sex, a small taboo-breaking, which presents sexuality as unproblematic – compared with Jimmy and Alison's fraught sexuality.

Beatie is caught between two worlds (herself a 'bridge'), the sophisticated London world of Ronnie and his friends, and home in the country, where she fits immediately as soon as she gets back, helping Jenny with domestic tasks.

The motif of men's physical vulnerability is also present in an old neighbour, Stan, who messes his pants and whom Jimmy hoses down. Caring between men is represented as something which is an automatic part of social responsibility both here and in *Chicken Soup* when Ronnie looks after his father after the stroke, implying gentle moments where domestic gender roles are subverted.

Beatie is preparing a party to welcome Ronnie to the family. There is a positive recognition of the gender bias in this play represented in its action, much of which is housework. This is both backdrop and content, with housework presented as valid action in its own right – but even here Ronnie intervenes on this traditionally female territory. Ronnie, a professional chef, has been teaching Beatie to cook, and she uses his recipe for a sponge cake. The food symbolism is continually double-edged; it gives the women pleasure to prepare, it satisfies and nurtures their families, but it is also the area in which the men have pain. When Beatie's father comes in, he has stomach-ache. (Another man enters female territory and is ill.)

In Act Three the family gathers to wait for Ronnie. A letter from him arrives, saying the relationship won't work and that he has decided not to come. The action builds to the final coda; it is evident that all the things that Beatie has been arguing about with her family are really externalised versions of what was going on within her – the play is really about the struggle within her own consciousness, between two different kinds of individual and social future, and Ronnie has merely acted as an *agent provocateur* – a device to catalyse her awakening. Beatie needs to plead and argue for her own family to support her:

> Your daughter's been ditched. It's your problem as well, isn't it? I'm part of your family, aren't I? Well, help me then! . . . Talk to me – for God's sake, someone talk to me.

Her mother suggests having tea, her father doesn't know. There is a confrontation between Beatie and her mother, and a mother/daughter confrontation is something very rare in both contemporary and historical drama. Beatie's speech, about the nature of her social displacement and the importance of understanding one's roots, comes out of this conflict as a resolution for her own consciousness: 'The things that make you proud of yourself – roots.' It is significant that for this speech she doesn't need to stand on a chair, as for the first time she is speaking for herself. She is a questing and questioning figure who is given a social significance beyond the simple rehabilitation of someone after a failed love affair:

> There are millions of us, all over the country, and no one, not one of us, is asking questions. We're all taking the easiest way out.

Beatie is now even able to mock Ronnie's idealised view of the Bryants 'living in mystic communion with Nature', since she knows the reality. She sees the apathy that makes it possible for consumerism to exploit people (an idea from Ronnie), and realises through this that she has given birth to her own voice, not to Ronnie's. For some of Ronnie's messages to have taken root in Beatie's consciousness, he has had to leave her. She is still as distanced from her own family as she has always been, she is still the restless person who went out to seek some alternative, but she is beginning to find her own voice. The final triumphant statement comes from the stage directions: 'As Beatie stands alone, articulate at last, the curtain falls.'

In both these plays, the family is a potent and real force. In both, Jewish and gentile, women are acknowledged as powerful centres of the family. This leads to a fascinating contradiction: on the one hand the women are given a powerful political and cultural voice which in most other plays is the prerogative of men. On the other hand, the conventional gender roles within the family are seen to be under strain. This is shown not just through social change (Ada and Dave moving away, Beatie leaving home) but through the way the male breadwinner is undermined by physical incapacity, and it is men who are shown as physically disintegrating. The explicit content of the plays celebrates the potency of women's cultural voice, while its symbolic subtext embodies the question of whether the articulation of the female voice implies the damaging or silencing of the male voice. In addition, the independent female voice seems to need to be free of male ties: Sarah, through Harry's disintegration; Beatie, at the end of a relationship; and in the next play, Cissie and Esther.

I'm Talking About Jerusalem, the third play in the trilogy, was also first performed in Coventry in 1960. It dovetails in time in and out of the two previous plays, filling in gaps and giving us information and insight into things that happened during the years in which the previous works are set.

It opens in Norfolk in the late 1940s, when Ada and Dave first move in. Again, a domestic scene with the mother as central, is presented at the very beginning. Sarah is buttering bread. Ronnie is standing on a box conducting the gramophone. The time is post-war with the return of the Labour Party, but ironically Ada and Dave, in the face of new progress and lifestyles, are going back in time: they have no electricity or running water, there are no roads, and no proper lavatory in this rural 'utopia'. But because the whole family is cooperating in the move, the mood is happy and active. Ronnie is an articulate and witty Jimmy Porter, shouting his slogans:

> Down with capitalism! Long live the workers' revolution . . . And long live Ronnie Kahn too!

25

Sarah has brought bottled chicken soup, echoing the title of the first play of the trilogy.

Ada counters Ronnie's passionate belief in the importance of words: 'Because we talk about one thing and you hear another, that's why', as if different people's ideas cannot be mediated through language. There is also now an opposition between town and country. For Dave the ideal of manhood has been 'emasculated' by city life and by the kind of alienated labour available to him. 'All their humanity gone. These you call men.' This leads him to choose a William-Morris lifestyle based on craft. He wants his work and his family to be one, but he is choosing a different route back to the old values which Sarah espouses so passionately. They are living out their ideals in practice, but this upsets Sarah who feels Ada has moved too far away.

In Act Two, Dave's RAF friend Libby is visiting them, and Ada is pregnant. Libby is not Jewish; he is a cynic and jeers at the back-to-nature move, accusing Dave and Ada of being individualists. He does, in a moment of vulnerability, acknowledge: '. . . of course I believe in Jerusalem, only I personally can't measure up to it'. Libby also has a very different attitude to women from that implicit in the lives of the other characters. He warns Dave:

> A woman dirties you up as well, you know. She and the world – they change you, they bruise you, they dirty you up – between them, you'll see.

When he describes the woman he was married to, he recalls Jimmy Porter's attitude:

> She's the kind that dirties you up. There was I sharing out my wealth, and there was she – always wanting to possess things, terrified of being on her own. She marries a man in order to have something to attach to herself, a possession! The man provides a home – bang! She's got another possession. *Her* furniture, *her* saucepans, *her* kitchen – bang, bang, bang! Then she has a baby – bang, again. All possessions! And this is the way she grows. She grows and she grows and she grows, and she takes from a man all the things she once loved him for – so that no one else can have them . . . I think I hate women because they have no vision . . .

This is a misogyny never expressed by any of the Jewish characters. Libby is somebody who has perhaps not had the benefit of an intimate family life where women can have aspirations. He feels free to express his misogyny through words, while Harry retreats into silence, manifesting his unhappiness in part through physical symptoms. That Harry contains unexpressed rage is clear when we learn that he had to be put in a padded cell after a second stroke.

The play moves to 1956, and Cissie and Esther, two aunts, visit Dave and Ada. These are two single women, vigorous, energetic and chirpy, producing a faintly comic double act between them, Cissie the political activist.

The utopia, which Ada and Dave had hoped to find in the country, has proved to have its own problems. Dave's furniture making does not produce enough money and he has trouble with the man who originally employed him. Personal life and social ideals are again under stress. In the middle of this Esther and Cissie talk and argue affectionately, showing that communication between people is a sign of love, of survival. Dave and Ada decide to return to London, Dave still holding on to his vision, to start a new workshop.

As 1959 shows a slip in the Labour Party's popularity, Ronnie becomes sadder, perhaps not exactly cynical but a little wistful for ideals which no longer seem to hold. There is a very touching description of the way he looked after Harry before he died, cementing the gender bonds between father and son. And Ronnie begins to realise that words themselves have certain limitations:

As soon as I say something, somehow I don't believe it . . . as soon as you pronounce something it doesn't seem true.

Ada and Dave believe in putting ideals into practice, whereas for Ronnie, ideals and language are still paramount. He does, however, still acknowledge the presence and necessity of Sarah as the centre of the family: 'Well, Sarah – your children are coming home now.' And although the play exemplifies the pain of the visions that keep people going and how difficult it is to live them out, there is a kind of determined optimism in Ronnie's last shout: 'We must be bloody mad to cry.'

The Wesker trilogy is unique in post-war British drama in the way it seamlessly intersects political vision and family life. It is interesting that it does so through the lives of a Jewish family, who see themselves as entirely assimilated, and yet still carry many of their Jewish cultural features with them, in the passionate intensity with which politics are argued and personal/family life defended. The nature of the relationship between Jewishness and the dominant culture is exemplified in both social and gender terms: Ronnie hovers behind *Roots*, influencing a gentile woman (the Old Testament behind the New?), Beatie wins through to a personal–feminist victory, but still accepts Ronnie's ideas. Libby's 'Porterish' cynicism in *I'm Talking* is trounced by the values of Jewish family life, and yet this family life is under strain. The fragmented time structure of *Jerusalem* in relation to the other two plays in its very form reflects the growing fragmentedness of family life as politics and personal life change and as the simple anti-fascist urgencies of the 1930s move into the far greater political complexities of the late 1950s.

The domestic settings concentrate on things that are often considered to be trivial: housework, cooking, the practical craft of day to day survival, devalued because it is considered largely to be women's work. Also, a woman is at the centre of much of the conceptual force of the drama, a Jewish woman. To the dominant British culture this may appear a minority or outsider point of view. Statistically, of course, Jews are a minority group. Sarah, the custodian of political and personal values, is a double outsider: she is Jewish and a woman. Just as Jimmy Porter could be seen as the outsider spokesman for his generation, so Sarah and the Kahn family can be seen to be expressing something very important about socialist ideals and the state of the family in pre- and post-war British society.

In the Wesker trilogy, sexuality as explicit subject matter is either absent, (ie the children are too young, the older people are too old, there are single women) or it is unproblematic. If anything, the sexual is one of the simplest and most enjoyable parts of Beatie's and Ronnie's relationship. Sexuality does not enter into the arena of conflict and contradiction, unlike the two Osborne plays in which sexuality is at the core of the playwright's concern.

It would be too crude to say that the taboos on the direct physical expression of sexuality on stage displaced the concern for it on to a concern for emotion expressed through language. But all five plays do have in common a preoccupation with the idea of expressing emotion and ideas through language in their desire to make sense of post-war society and shifting gender roles. They are all so vigorously wordy that the silence of Alison and Harry takes on even greater significance. It appears certainly that the articulacy of one sex must always be at the expense of the other.

The State, Communication and Gender

Waiting for Godot by Samuel Beckett

The Room and *The Birthday Party*
by Harold Pinter

The next three plays are stylistically different from the realism of Osborne and Wesker. *Waiting for Godot* by Samuel Beckett was first performed in England in 1955 as a full club performance because the censor demanded a number of textual cuts, in which anything sexual or excretory related to the lower part of the body was to be excised. The cast of five are referred to by male pronouns, and the stage directions state that four (not the Boy) wear bowler hats. Vladimir and Estragon have a close relationship, and on occasions they talk like a double act.

As well as carrying subtle philosophical questions about the meaning of existence, the text touches in a more expressionist and symbolic way on the kind of comment that Sarah Kahn makes in the Wesker Trilogy about the welfare state bureaucracy. The ritualistic dialogue, and the ritual city-gent appearance symbolised by the bowler hats, are ways of reflecting on the intervention of bureaucracy into people's personal lives, through the faceless men (sic) of the ministries – an irony, since the welfare state's intention was to enhance the possibilities for individual and personal pleasure and comfort.

All the characters are waiting for Godot, who is designated as 'he', an absent figure who embodies the values by which these people live, but to whom they do not have access. The nameless Boy, like an innocent Greek messenger, brings the truth that Godot is coming tomorrow.

Here the all-male rituals create a non-realistic world, without any recognisable social institution to give them shape. Here is no army, no city; just men trying to find comradeship, but coming up only with rituals which lack meaning and vision. It is a play without a consciousness of history, with men represented as outcasts, whose relationships mirror the symbiotic relations of marriage: Estragon and Vladimir don't know why they are together, but they know they can't do without one another. Pozzo and his servant Lucky conduct a titillatory master/slave relationship where Lucky is reduced to an animal.

There are no women in the play although associations with women occasionally appear in the form of some of the sexual references. The absence of women frees the men into a semi-pornographic homo-eroticism. There is a section about Vladimir buttoning his fly, and chat about erections (objects of the censor's blue pencil). There is some pulling up and down of trousers, and talk about embracing. Through the stream of consciousness and surrealism, emerge some of the themes already discussed: male association and a quest for meaning in today's world. But the terrain is featureless, the meanings controlled by an invisible authority which leaves the men locked in symbolic relationships which they cannot control. The modern state, it seems, produces a parody of marriage instead of male bonding, and reduces men from sexually potent beings to sinister beings who can only ring the changes on semi-pornographic power relations. Only the nameless Boy is free of these 'sins', embodying a romantic moment of symbolic hope.

Where *Waiting for Godot* has elliptical and elusive allusions to the 'real' world, Harold Pinter bridges the social realism of the first plays discussed and the distanced surrealism of Beckett. *The Room* and *The Birthday Party* are notable for the ordinariness of their titles and the comforting simplicity of their references, suggesting family and domesticity.

The Room was first performed in 1957, and we are back in the bed-sitting room. There is a gas stove, a sink and a double bed. All domestic personal functions, except those of the lavatory, are seen on stage. Rose opens the play, feeding Bert with bacon and eggs, establishing the image of the nurturing mother. Rose appears to be in charge of her own territory.

According to Rose, people feel safe in their own homes; it is from this security she can be curious about all outsiders, who constitute a threat. But unlike the worlds of *Look Back* and the Wesker trilogy, here home is not what it seems. Rose has a landlord, and the home which means everything to her does not belong to her. Rose's main fear is that someone will come and take her room, and so great is her fear that she never goes out. Bert, her husband, comes and goes, and is free to be active in the outside world. He speaks of the van he controls as 'she', in contrast to Rose's function in the room where she is in control of what goes on, although not in control of its structure.

One of the characteristics of Pinter's dialogue is that people appear to speak in an almost childlike manner. They say simple things, as if learning to talk, learning to express themselves; recalling the importance of verbal expression in all the ways discussed so far (although realised here in a very different style). In a very real way the play is about the act of struggle to communicate, and people do understand each other within the verbal world which Pinter creates, even if the dialogue often seems to glance off the person to whom it is addressed. But the sense of repetition and ritual in the dialogue represents emotional anxiety, a personal kind of insecurity with people obsessed by their own concerns, and this has important implications in terms of gender.

There is a man in the basement, whom Rose fears; he is Riley, a blind 'negro'. Even though he is an outsider, black, incapacitated, he is still a man, and he represents fear of the unknown to Rose.

At the end the real power relations are revealed: Bert acquires the power of speech and controls events in the room. Rose's insecurity is real, and the only action is taken by Bert. Rose is revealed as a kind of helpless mother who performs all the nurturing activities powerlessly in the room, which she does not control, while outside lurks an alien 'child' figure.

The Birthday Party, first staged in 1958, is also set in a living room, but the domestic functions are more dispersed; there is a hatch to the kitchen. Again, the play starts with Petey being served with food by Meg, the mother image dominating. We have another odd 'family' in which the child figure is Stanley, the lodger, with a rather sinister and uncomfortable relationship to Meg, who teases and flirts with him. She treats him both as a little boy and as an adult sexual male. Stanley rejects her advances violently.

The boarding-house setting signifies a milieu in transit; events are catalysed by the outsider figures of McCann and Goldberg who is Jewish. There are many moments in which McCann and Goldberg could almost be characters out of a Beckett play wandering by chance onto another stage. Petey has met them and told them they could stay. As in Beckett, there is some vague sense of an official role; they refer to their 'job', using semi-military words like 'assignment' and 'mission'.

When Meg says that it is Stanley's birthday, Goldberg and McCann decide to give him a party – more outsiders who come in and decide what is to happen in Meg's house, on the woman's territory, as in *The Room*. The only other woman in the play is the dolly-bird figure of Lulu, and like Meg she has no real power in relationships or on the territory. She is merely sexual.

At the beginning of Act One Petey sits reading a newspaper, and at the beginning of Act Two McCann sits tearing a newspaper into equal strips. This harks back to the reading of the newspapers in *Look Back* – the newspapers belong to the men, symbolising their access to the outside world.

There are problems about being touched. McCann doesn't want Stanley to touch his arm, echoing the desire to express emotion but the fear of physical contact in *Waiting for Godot*, with the concept of censorship internalised in the dramatic action itself. The verbal and physical assaults on Stanley from McCann and Goldberg are open to a number of different kinds of interpretation, one of which is that he has no history and he does not belong to anyone or anywhere, to no family, and is therefore dangerous and fair game. Goldberg's ironic speech carries a serious undertone about a break between past and present values:

> What's happened to the love, the bonhomie, the unashamed expression of affection of the day before yesterday, that our Mums taught us in the nursery . . . We all wander on our tod through this world. It's a lonely pillow to kip on.

McCann and Goldberg finally take Stanley away, after a choric litany of how they are going to help him and make him more integrated. Stanley is reduced to jibberish: he has forgotten how to talk, to use language, to control his view of the world. Petey tries vainly to stop the process. Meg then returns and chatters on about the party. Petey doesn't tell her what has happened and pretends that Stanley is still upstairs in bed, keeping her in ignorance. This reiterates the paradox of the woman being powerless on her own territory. Meg is totally excluded from the central power struggle between Stanley and the two outsiders. She has the power to feed and nurture but not to make any decisions about the nature of power relationships. Given the 'family' set-up at the beginning of the play with the two 'parents' having breakfast while waiting for the 'son' to come downstairs, by implication we have witnessed the world taking a son from a mother, who may be sexually dangerous to him, but is nevertheless very important. Just as things often work in the conventional family, father (Petey) is allowed to understand, but mother (Meg) must be 'protected' from this knowledge. Meg is powerless not just in terms of material control but also in terms of what she is allowed to know about the world's processes.

None of this detracts in any way from the strange, sinister power games which are played between the men, which we see, whereas we do not see the same processes happening in relation to either Meg or Lulu. The women do not contribute in any significant way to the chief dynamic of the play, and function largely as types – mother and dolly-bird. We have a male-centred and male-focussed action on what appears at first to be female territory; the domestic.

This provides a new perspective if we see the Beckett and the Pinter plays as in part about the nature of an obscure authority controlling the values by which people live – the state, perceived imaginatively through the disorder of some men's lives and the powerlessness of women. But within this bewildering personal world, with the family models which hover behind Beckett and Pinter, there are small-scale power compensations for the men, who control the domestic territory and the relations within it. Sexuality is repressed (Beckett) or fraught (Pinter), and the latter explores further a displaced Oedipal relationship, in which the 'mother' figure is given a precarious compensatory moment of sexual power over the 'son', functioning also as a fantasy figure for him. These themes appear again in the late 1960s stage world of Joe Orton.

Militarism and the Outside World

Serjeant Musgrave's Dance by John Arden

Of the fifteen characters in *Serjeant Musgrave's Dance* (first performed at the Royal Court in 1959) two are women, and in his introduction John Arden says:

> I would suggest that a study of the roles of the women and of Private Attercliffe should be sufficient to remove any doubts as to where the 'moral' of the play lies.

The author clearly intended the minority sex to carry the weight of the play's moral, and this might suggest that the role of the women will be central to the action of the play. However, it is clear early on that the social milieu which the play explores is that of the army and the colliery, both of which are male territories.

The soldiers under Serjeant Musgrave are a group with a tradition and a hierarchy. As Musgrave says: 'We have our duty. A soldier's duty is a soldier's life.' The four soldiers have arrived in a town with a mining strike, apparently to recruit. Musgrave's authority over the soldiers is counterpointed by the local parson who also happens to be a magistrate, so that his authority covers both religion and secular law and order in the town.

The two women are introduced in a public house run by Mrs Hitchcock, in which Annie is the barmaid. Annie sleeps with soldiers, and is defensively bitter and cynical about them:

> What good's a bloody soldier, except to be dropped into a slit in the ground like a letter in a box.

Mrs Hitchcock comments on the local situation calmly and objectively:

> No work in the colliery, the owner calls it a strike, the men call it a lock-out, we call it starvation.

The mayor, a local functionary, also owns the colliery.

Musgrave, to all intents and purposes, is a straightforward and decent man – he reads a pocket Bible and promises that there will be

34

no drunkenness and no fornication from his soldiers. We learn that a local boy, Billy Hicks, got Annie pregnant, and then went off to the army and was killed, and that Annie gave birth to a deformed child which died. One evident function of Annie's role is already set up in juxtaposition with the military values conveyed by the soldiers and Musgrave. Annie is a victim of the cruelty of war, not only because her lover was killed, but symbolically because the child she has given birth to is emblematic of deformities which militarism and soldiering can produce. Motherhood functions in a real way for Annie: as a loss which she mourns realistically as a woman, and she is a symbolic extension of the values which the men dramatically enact.

The truth soon emerges that the soldiers are deserters, and Musgrave has stolen some money. But even so, Musgrave still has an authority over them: 'My power is the power of God.' The soldiers have come to the town because of Billy; Sparky, one of the soldiers, was his friend, and the solidarity, loyalty and honour between him and Billy is his passionate motive for returning. Musgrave's motive is both more extravagant and dangerous; it is a return to expiate the sin of Billy's death as some kind of crusade: '. . . their rights and our war are the same one corruption.' For Musgrave the crusade is for God.

Not one of the play's scenes is set in a private home. The public house is one of the social centres of the town, a relatively neutral area where the men can meet. In the public house women serve men with drink and food as an extension of their domestic role, with Mrs Hitchcock presiding as a neutral mother figure.

Musgrave sees women as dangerous, their sexuality confusing and getting in the way of the righteous crusade he is waging:

> . . . There's work for women and there's work for men: and let the two get mixed, you've anarchy.

He warns Annie off the men: 'You will not stand between them and their strength.'

Annie comes to the stable where the men sleep, and there is some rivalry over whom she is going to sleep with. Hurst breaks away from her: 'You want me to lose my life inside of you' – echoing the Jimmy Porter fear of female sexuality. Although, of all the characters in the play, Annie is the one with the least social power, the 'outsider' from within, as it were, it is precisely her wildness and

35

iconoclasm which seems to produce fear in the men. Annie comments ironically: 'I'm a whore to the soldiers – it's a class by itself.' Attercliffe grabs at her crudely and violently, kisses her and then tells a bitter story about how his wife slept with the greengrocer. Annie and Sparky, however, perhaps recognising some kind of similar alienation in each other, embrace with passion. Meanwhile Musgrave is plagued by nightmares, Mrs Hitchcock comes to wake him up, brings him hot grog – again, a woman consoling him, serving him – and covers him up, soothing him back to sleep: a benevolent and non-sexual mother soothing a boy with a bad dream. The women here too are divided between two types – the mother and the whore.

In the stables there is a brawl, in which Sparky is accidentally killed. Attercliffe is left holding the bayonet. In the context of Arden's opening comment, Attercliffe is seen as a victim who against his intentions and better judgement has accidentally killed a man. However, there is a very important difference between Attercliffe and Annie: Attercliffe is part of the central male grouping from the beginning, and therefore as well as his symbolic importance as the victim of the group – a different kind of victim from Sparky – he is always an active part of the central action; while Annie remains on the outside of the action, drawn in only when necessary. After Sparky's death she is removed from the action; she is in a state of shock, with blood on her hands, and Musgrave tells Mrs Hitchcock to take Annie and lock her up. Mrs Hitchcock accepts his authority without question, and the audience too has to take it for granted, since Annie and Mrs Hitchcock have no real stage relationship independent of the men.

Act Three begins in the market place, a public space, where Musgrave plays devil's advocate arguing for the beauty of the gun and its power to kill; in order to shock the local population. There is a skeleton dressed as a soldier which Musgrave dances around ghoulishly claiming the bones are those of Billy Hicks. Musgrave's version of a holy revenge is that twenty-five people must die in return for the accidental and violent death of Billy Hicks. Attercliffe accuses Musgrave of betrayal, since he believed that this was a genuine crusade to end all killing.

Musgrave orders Mrs Hitchcock to bring Annie back. Annie makes a very simple speech, sadness at having lost her love, and here she functions as a tart-turned-Ophelia – an innocent who has been driven literally mad. While the soldiers talk about being mad, they still have a logic and motivations. In Annie's case, however, her most potent statements are made through song, through the emotion of music and the imagery of the words. This reinforces her as the most potent symbolic figure in the play, but again it is at the expense of any integration with the other characters and the central action. Attercliffe, on the other hand, is still involved with the other men. Annie, as she cradles the skeleton, presents a chilling and empty mother image, which echoes the loss of her own dead baby, and defines her motherhood in relation to deformed and murderous men in the army. At the end of the play it is Mrs Hitchcock who comes to Attercliffe and Musgrave in prison with comfort and port and lemon, a maternal go-between who doesn't take sides: although she does tell Musgrave at the end that he's got it all wrong, her message is impersonal since we have not seen her real response to events since the arrival of the soldiers. Mrs Hitchcock is non-sexual, just a mother figure. Annie is sexual, and problematically so; her sexuality is castigated in the context of the play and punished. She functions in Jack Musgrave's fantasy as a sexually dangerous woman, but it is interesting that the play's dramatic crisis is precipitated after a scene in which sexual contact between Annie and the men has actually happened, as if in imaginative justification of Musgrave's fear about the intervention of women, and an echo of the crisis in *A Patriot* after Redl has sexual relations with the Countess. The women have to be marginalised, and literally atomised – Annie is locked up – from the action and contained in their gender function in order to be potent as dramatic and moral symbols. There is a sense in which the women could be cut out of the play and its chief messages would not be fundamentally altered. They would simply have to be written into relations between the men.

Annie, it is worth noting, is a double outsider. She is not just outside the central action because the army is all-male, but she is an outsider in her own community because she is seen as a prostitute and goes with soldiers. This makes her both doubly castigated, and something of a tragic figure.

The play is essentially about power relations, morality, values, militarism and violence, as they are enacted between men. As in *A Patriot*, the play moves between different territories and spaces, in keeping with the mobility of an army, very much a public play. But whereas in *A Patriot* the personal relationships are represented as interwoven with the public relationships, in *Musgrave* the personal relationships are secondary and symbolic so that even the Annie/ Billy relationship is something that has happened in the past. The engagement between characters is on the basis of shared public functions and conflicting public dilemmas. This is a more overtly selfconscious public political piece, in which sexuality has only a symbolic role.

Given the marginality of the women to the realistic action, they are not only brought on and taken off by demand, but they are also separated from each other, both in the sense that Mrs Hitchcock is Annie's boss, and also in that they have no scenes together. The moral issues are shown only as of personal relevance to men in public places. Women, in this epic landscape, remain imaginatively dangerous if sexual, and merely instrumental if maternal. But either way, their power as symbols is enhanced by excluding them from the theatrical dynamic, from serious interaction with either the male characters or each other. Politics and moral issues are presented as 'male' concerns, in contrast to a figure such as Sarah Kahn, and the personal is therefore separated from the political, except insofar as it is symbolically useful.

Motherhood and Masculinity

A Taste of Honey by Shelagh Delaney;
The Sport of My Mad Mother and *The Knack*
by Ann Jellicoe

The next play returns to a domestic setting – 'a comfortless flat in Manchester'. *A Taste of Honey* by Shelagh Delaney (Theatre Royal Stratford, May 1958, directed by Joan Littlewood), is set in Salford in Lancashire. Helen, the mother, is described as 'a semi-whore', and she and her daughter Jo share with the audience an unfamiliarity with the stage environment. The first dialogue presents a mother and daughter entwined in conflict, a different situation from the plays discussed so far, where mothering is either assumed, as with Sarah Kahn and Mrs Hitchcock, or used as a symbolic vehicle. Here motherhood itself is a central theme. The relationship between Helen and Jo is the reverse of what one normally expects: Jo, the daughter, is the more responsible of the two. There is an uncomfortable intimacy between the two of them, exacerbated by the fact that they have to share a bed.

Where the Wesker trilogy shows a family fragmenting over a period of twenty-odd years, here we see an already fragmented family. This mother and daughter are displaced from family life and in lodgings, like the characters in the Pinter plays. Helen comments wryly on the changes between generations:

> You bring them up and they turn round and talk to you like that. I would never have dared talk to my mother like that when I was her age. She'd have knocked me into the middle of next week.

Jo is planning to leave school, and wants to get away from her mother. The dialogue between her and Helen is a familiar ritual and the two of them are used to a nomadic existence. Helen's boyfriend Peter arrives, and Jo is cynical about him: 'What's this one called?' Helen is also cynical about men but obviously can't do without them. There is some sexual banter between Helen and Peter, and here we have a significant departure: Helen, the mother of a grown-up daughter, has a very visible and active sexuality, likes drinking, and has her own life. In the process, however, she neglects her daughter's interests, and does not behave like a 'good' mother:

JO: You should prepare my meals like a proper mother.
HELEN: Have I ever laid claim to being a proper mother?'

But she is at least allowed the space to have vigour, motherhood and sexuality. The appearance of motherhood as subject matter (an 'outsider' subject?) breaks an unspoken taboo on theatrical content, which in the vast majority of plays is defined by issues of direct concern to men. The gender bias in this play is also reversed from that of most other plays, in that it is the women we follow from scene to scene. The men come and go according to the needs of the women characters.

In the second scene another taboo is broken; Jo's boyfriend is 'a coloured naval rating', doing his National Service – another outsider, who carries none of the sinister overtones of Pinter's Riley. Interestingly, the boyfriend in the cast list is simply designated as 'Boy', as if the taboo can only be partially broken by leaving him unnamed, and therefore unindividualised.

The conversations are gritty, painful and very honest. Helen and Peter decide to get married and go away on honeymoon. Jo, who is still a child in many ways, feels abandoned. Although Helen's sexuality is presented as unproblematic – she is old enough to know what she is doing and to enjoy it as well – Jo's sexuality is more delicately and ambiguously treated. The boy stays with her over Christmas. A brief exchange encapsulates the sexual ambiguities:

JO: Don't do that.
BOY: Why not?
JO: I like it.

There is a painful conversation between Helen and Jo on Helen's wedding day when Jo wants to know about her father, and Helen says that he was retarded. Jo is illegitimate from a one-night stand and Helen, despite her determination to live her life as she wants it, still wishes for something different for her daughter. She says to Jo: 'Why don't you learn from my mistakes?' Both Helen and Jo are desperate for affection but are unable to give it to one another.

In Act Two, Jo is pregnant – a real event, integral to the life, thought, feeling and action of the character. Geof, a young gay man

– another outsider looking for affection – moves in with Jo, and Jo frankly admits his difference: 'I've always wanted to know about people like you.' Geof is ambiguous about women: 'I can't stand women at times.' He quickly becomes a substitute mother, looking after Jo, preparing the cot and the clothes for the baby. Geof has no active sexuality, like Cliff in *Look Back*. He doesn't mention lovers – he doesn't seem to want or need any; he seems perfectly satisfied by the mothering role he takes on in relation to Jo. He is very much more 'maternal' than Jo, who claims: 'I hate babies.' The expected gender roles are continually being subverted: Jo, the young pregnant girl, has no interest in babies; she is a woman rebelling against motherhood and biological destiny. Geof, the gay man, actually has all the feelings she is meant to have. Jo comments: 'It comes natural to you . . . you'd make somebody a wonderful wife.' Jo struggles against growing up into womanhood and motherhood, her fears expressed quite honestly, when she talks about breastfeeding: 'I'm not having a little animal nibbling away at me, it's cannibalistic. Like being eaten alive.'

The relationship between Jo and Geof has an openness precisely because it is free from any kind of sexual trammels. They do try and have a physical relationship (Geof admitting that he has never kissed a girl), but Jo gets angry, saying she doesn't 'enjoy all this panting and grunting'. She and Geof do, however, construct a comfortable and reassuring home together in a non-sexual, semi-role-reversed 'marriage'. As in *Look Back*, real affection appears possible only without sexuality. Jo says, 'I always want to have you with me, because I know you'll never ask anything from me.' She can make no distinction between sex and love: 'I'm sick of love.' Jo holds Geof's hand and says:

> I used to try and hold my mother's hands, but she always used to pull them away from me . . . She had so much love for everyone else, but none for me.

But when Geof gets Jo a doll on which to practise, she turns fearful and violent:

> I'll bash its brains out. I'll kill it. I don't want his baby, Geof. I don't want to be a mother. I don't want to be a woman.

Interestingly it is only at this point that we actually learn that the boy whose baby Jo is carrying is called Jimmy, and it is telling that the character mentions his name, as if at one remove from the author.

Helen returns when Peter throws her out, and Jo welcomes her back:

. . . For the first time in my life I feel really important. I feel as though I could take care of the whole world.

Motherhood feels possible when her own mother is there, however complex the mother/daughter relationship is. Helen behaves appallingly to Geof, who, until he finally leaves, always has Jo's interests at heart. He is presented as a good and generous person – a positive and taboo-breaking view of a male homosexual, but one who can only be unproblematic because his homosexuality is strictly off-stage. In the end there is something very poignant in Jo and Geof's inability to make any long-lasting statement about their friendship and affection for each other. As soon as Geof leaves, Jo and Helen revert to their old sniping relationship, particularly when Jo tells Helen that the baby might be black.

The characters have little trouble expressing very real and painful feelings, and perhaps this is because they are all in one sense or another socially marginal – single mother and part-time whore, illegitimate teenage mother, gay white man, black sailor boy.

Sexuality is problematical for Helen, Jo and Geof, as is motherhood. Geof's inclination to 'mother' Jo and her impending baby can be represented, but in the end it cannot be validated; the 'natural' rights intervene, and the mother/daughter relationship, however fraught, overrides any other kind of chosen relationship – even that between Geof and Jo which is based on real friendship.

While the play breaks a number of sexual and racial taboos, in the end it is the old values, however dislocated, which rule – the values of blood relationships between generations of women. The dilemma is that motherhood is forced upon some women, and some men are denied the chance to nurture. The dilemmas are real and not displaced onto other causes or characters. The family of women appears to be the one constant factor, but even that is fraught, placing the strains squarely within personal life. The core emotional relationship is that between mother and daughter; motherhood is explored unsentimentally, even at times brutally.

Female sexuality and motherhood are shown in symbiotic and problematic relationship, and in this play two significant departures are marked: the territory is largely domestic, and the dramatic action is controlled by the women. The gender dynamics are female-centred, and women are centrally placed as subject matter.

The Sport of My Mad Mother, by Ann Jellicoe, was first performed in 1958. In a preface written in 1964, Jellicoe says that the play was:

> . . . not written intellectually according to a pre-arranged plan. It was shaped bit by bit until the bits felt right in relation to each other and to the whole. It is an anti-intellect play, not only because it is about irrational forces and urges, but because one hopes it will reach the audience directly through rhythm, noise and music and their reaction to basic stimuli.

This alludes to the use of ritual repetition, characters as a kind of chorus, a more heightened ritualistic form of some of the styles that Pinter was using. Jellicoe is aware of the social meaning of ritual:

> We create rituals when we want to strengthen, celebrate or define our common life or common values, or when we want to give ourselves confidence to undertake a common course of action.

There is a connection between the formal ways in which she aimed to affect her audience's emotions, and the ways in which writers such as Delaney and Wesker were trying to write about the expression of feeling in relationships between people. Jellicoe continues:

> Most of the people in the play distrust emotion and haven't the means to express it anyway, and they tend to say things which they think will sound good. But at the same time they betray their real feeling either by what they do or by the very fact that they need to assume a mask.

Jellicoe sets up a contradiction between the conscious level of expression through the dialogue and the unconscious demonstration of meaning on stage through movement, gesture and rhythm. Jellicoe also homes in on myth:

> *The Sport of My Mad Mother* is concerned with fear and rage at being rejected from the womb or tribe. It uses a very old myth in which a man, rejected by his mother, castrates himself with a stone knife.

The figure of the mother has appeared as all-powerful in Wesker, as sexually destructive in Osborne, as sinister in Pinter, as servicing and symbolic in Arden, under real investigation in Delaney. In all except the last the definition of virility, what it is to be male viewed from the perspective of the male, seems to involve the imaginative solution of the male distancing himself from the concept of the mother, particularly when there is any danger that sexuality and motherhood might merge. Ann Jellicoe takes an opposite myth as her conceptual departure point. Unlike the men, who seem to need to reject and destroy the mother imaginatively in order to become a man, the power relations here are reversed – the man is rejected by his mother.

The Sport of My Mad Mother is more explicitly about the concept of gender roles than any of the other plays so far discussed. This might seem paradoxical given its very free-associative and ritualistic form. But this very abstraction liberates the imagination to conceptualise roles.

At the beginning Steve arrives with percussion instruments, and he remains onstage during the interval. This has a double significance: it maintains a sense of theatrical illusion, and it is also reassuring. Steve remains as a link between the audience and the hermetic ritualistic world which the stage characters inhabit. Because of his link with music Steve is a personification of the unconscious onstage, always there as part of the action.

There are three women and four men, a group of young people hanging around with nothing to do. Patty is described as 'a pretty little cockney girl with a lot of make-up round her eyes', conventionally feminine in the fashion of the day. The male characters have odd names such as 'Fak' and 'Cone', that deliberately depersonalise them. A kind of collective unconscious speaks through the fragmentations of different individuals, creating a choric violence. There is a very conventional division of labour in the kinds of 'toys' that the male and female characters have: the boys play with guns; Patty has curlers and a home perm kit. The ritual of sexual chatting-up is echoed in verbal repetition, and it is mocked by being made into a theatrical device. Patty keeps having to be reminded by the others what she has done and where she has been, as if she has no identity until others give it to her.

Patty makes a very long speech about the still absent Greta (the absent mother?):

I wish I was Greta . . . Like spit on a hot plate, that's her . . . anyone'll do anything for her.

There is a sense of her power offstage as there is with Godot and

44

with Ronnie in the Wesker trilogy. Onstage it is Patty who is feminine, passive and powerless, and the boys, who wield power, however futile, to the point of being prepared to threaten one another with actual violence.

The figure of Dodo enters, who is 'either very young or very old'. Dodo is female, wearing a man's overcoat and making animal noises. In this one character are compressed a whole series of symbols and signs which subvert the very idea of fixed roles, male or female, old or young, innocent or sinister. Dodo has no social identity, and therefore no language: she speaks either single words or single syllables.

Act Two begins with the cast running around on the stage with sparklers in a kind of childlike celebration ritual. Dean, an American, attempting to perm Patty's hair, tries to make sense of the confusing instructions, which are repeated by everyone to the point where they make no sense at all, infuriating Patty. When the group dresses up in Dodo's old coats and blankets, Greta appears, dressed like the others so that she can mingle with them incognito. She speaks with an Australian accent. Dean tries to get hold of Greta, the two outsiders in some way trying to unite, perhaps the two parental figures trying to get together.

The stage directions state that when Greta moves away from the others 'the focus of action seems to go with her', and her power is continually demonstrated; she is a very theatrical figure, who produces fear and respect in her followers. When they all fall on Dean, Greta stops them with a word, then smashes a mug. When she beats Cone up, he loves every moment of it. Although the play is full of sudden violences, Greta's authority is always clear.

It is only at the end of the Act that Greta 'is seen to be pregnant'. The mother is first shown, therefore, in relation to her power over other people, and her pregnancy (i.e. her capacity to keep producing submissive followers) is made visible only as a moment of threat at the end of the Act. Her symbolic and potential motherhood are not presented as an alternative to her as a sexual being, since her relationships with the men have strong sexual undertones.

Act Three opens with everyone again waiting for Greta. Dean makes a long moral speech:

> Why be angry . . . I'm part of the human race and this waste – this violence – this degradation – it betrays humanity . . . If people will only have patience and intelligence and will power there's nothing we

can't master and control . . .

Meanwhile, the ritual violence continues, and in the process both Patty and Dodo reach a state of collapse.

Greta arrives and has a conversation with Dean about her hair. Dean says: 'And each Friday you dip it in blood – in human blood.' Greta answers: 'In baby's blood.' She continues:

> I was reared in a cave by a female wallaby. Until I was seven I ran about on all fours and barked.

She associates herself with the primitive, and there are echoes in the above exchange about baby's blood with the figure of Lilith who was reputed to be Adam's first wife and who was supposed to kill all her babies every day and then give birth to hundreds of new ones. The real confrontation in the play is between Dean and Greta, the two outsiders. Cone is jealous of Greta's pregnancy and fearful that she will reject him in favour of the new baby. Dean discourses on the need to be moral and kind, and then turns on Greta, who is in pain, perhaps in childbirth.

> You're not fit to have a child . . . You gross thing. Man/woman, cruel. Unstable. Frigid.

It is the men who fear the threat of Greta's power as mother and a sexual being. The Dean/Greta conflict is an elemental battle between two outsiders for territory, Greta representing the primitive, the animal and the sufferer, and Dean representing the thinker, the one who can talk about morality (a conventional division between feminine/masculine). Greta expresses this:

> Rails, rules, laws, guides, promises, terms . . . into the pot with the whole bloody lot. Birth. Birth. That's the thing. Oh, I shall have hundreds of children, millions of hundreds, and hundreds of millions.

She gives birth behind a sheet to a small white bundle. Cone bashes himself to death with a brick, while Greta examines the bundle. Steve, the musical mediator between action and audience, clears up.

Unlike *A Taste of Honey*, the mother figure is here explored from the point of view of its impact on the male characters. The men's imagination and fears dictate the way in which Greta is seen, and the way she sees herself. But unlike plays by some of the male playwrights already discussed, Greta does have real as well as symbolic power in her world. Greta actually gives birth, to something small and white (innocent?), and her power is expressed in her desire to give birth to hundreds and hundreds of children. This power is seen as sinister by the men, and Greta herself accepts this and defiantly flaunts the power of a woman who is both a mother and a sexual being.

The Knack, also by Ann Jellicoe, was first produced in 1961. This has four characters; three men and a woman. The men are precisely described both in terms of their physical appearance and the way they talk, but when it comes to the woman, Nancy, Jellicoe tells us how old she is (she is the only one who is given an age), but is vague about both her appearance and her way of speaking.

> Potentially a beautiful girl but her personality like her appearance is still blurred and unformed.

There is detail about the skirt she is to wear.

The play is set in a room which is in the process of being transformed by being painted. Both Jellicoe and Delaney demonstrate that work has to be put into a room before it can be lived in and maintained.

Tom is painting Colin's house. Although there is work going on, nobody seems very clear about its purpose. Here the absent person, whom everyone waits for and fears, is a character called Tolen. Tolen is out seeing a girl, and he arrives by motor bike. He is a macho man waiting for girls to phone. As Tom comments:

> He makes his contacts and stashes them up for later. He's enlarging his collection.

He goads Colin for not having a girl. Colin is obsessed by his own masculine limitations:

> How do you get a woman? How can I get a girl? . . . Why is Tolen so sexy?

Nancy appears first outside the window, i.e. outside the house, the men's territory. Colin wonders how long it takes Tolen to pick up a girl and make love to her. Tolen believes 'a man can develop the knack':

> First you must realise that women are not individuals, but types. No, not even types, just women. They want to surrender but they don't want the responsibility of surrendering. This is one reason why the

47

men must dominate . . . For you must appreciate, Colin, that people like to be dominated. They like to be mastered. They ask to be relieved of the responsibility of deciding for themselves . . . Very few men are real men, Colin, are real masters. Almost all women are servants . . .

Nancy again appears outside, this time with her luggage, looking for somewhere to stay, and Tolen demonstrates his 'knack' on this innocent outsider.

Act Two opens with Tom and Tolen painting. Nancy, who has just come to London, enters through the window. Tolen takes his belt off and chases her around the room, teasingly, but the undertones of sadism are clear enough, and Tom tries to protect her. Nancy begins to give in to Tolen, asking him for his approval, similar to the way in which Patty functions in the earlier play.

Like Jo in *Taste*, Nancy is ambivalent about sex: desiring and fearing it. Tom ties a sheet around her (there is a sheet also in *The Sport of My Mad Mother* – perhaps some sense that women have to be concealed, because of their associations with bed and sexuality). Colin is friendly and helpful towards Nancy but she doesn't respond to him, implying that his kind of gentle sexuality doesn't work, whereas Tolen's violent kind does.

As the action and the language become more frantic, Nancy claims she has been raped. Colin denies it, pointing out that the others have been there all the time. Tom then plays devil's advocate and says Tolen must rape Nancy because it's what she really wants. Nancy threatens to tell the police: the situation is surreal and sado-masochistic in that violence is always lurking but nobody quite knows how much has happened or been invited. The power balance is so much in favour of the men that it is difficult to see Nancy as anything other than an unwitting victim, and yet she does little to indicate that her passivity is not without some sense of invitation. By the end she is reduced to being able to utter only a single word 'rape'. There is finally a chase in which Tolen catches Nancy, then releases her and she goes to Colin. In the end Nancy chooses to go to the man who is sexually the least threatening.

Nancy is the isolated, token woman, the outsider new to the area – young, vulnerable, surrounded by men, and incapable of making decisions. She inspires sexual desires, and then doesn't know how to deal with them. There is a strong sense of collusion between her femininity and the men in the macho games they play. The ritualised and absurdist dialogue, together with the apparently randomly motivated action deployed by Jellicoe demonstrates this collusion, as well as satirising both the feminine and the macho.

Male sexuality is the centre of this play, with Colin and Tolen concerned with masculine sexual prowess and failure. The woman-as-collusive-victim is a secondary theme, which serves to illustrate certain assertions about male sexual types. Tolen's function as a representative of successful manhood is highlighted by his own comment: 'I have no first name. I never use my first name anyway', as if he has no individuality. Colin actually owns the house and yet he is subservient to the other two men, indicating that ownership and the characteristic of 'manliness' do not necessarily go together.

In these three plays, a shift in gender focus is evident: Delaney's play focuses on women as realistic subject matter, with their narrative demands determining the stage action, and with motherhood as a central theme. In both Jellicoe's plays, men remain the focal point of both form and content, and male sexuality is presented as the central dilemma. It is contained in an absurdist style which both reinforces and satirises the rituals of male sexuality, and by so doing forces a concentration on questions about sexual gender roles quite separately from any questions about gender difference at work, or political activism. As in Pinter, Delaney's characters are socially marginal, but make different gender points. As in Beckett, Jellicoe's characters are oddball, socially dislocated, inhabiting a non-real world, and her focus too differs from his in being very explicitly only about male sexuality, and implicitly about male/female roles.

Women and Emancipation

Each His (sic) Own Wilderness and
Play with a Tiger by Doris Lessing

Each His Own Wilderness (Royal Court, 1958) opens after 'an H bomb explosion'. Tony Bolton has just finished his National Service. He is described as resembling:

> . . . an adolescent girl who makes herself attractive as a form of self assertion, but is afraid when the attention she draws is more than gently chivalrous. . .

This suggests that Tony's bearing carries ambiguous implications for appropriately gendered behaviour.

At the core of this play is a volatile mother/son relationship, between Tony and his articulate politically-active mother, Myra. There are small subversive touches, such as the fact that Myra wears trousers, a little bit naughty in the late 1950s.

Tony craves more of his mother's affection, but Myra, in trying to control her own life and her relations with men and socialist politics seems to have to do so at the expense of her relationship with her son. Tony is jealous of Myra's young secretary Sandy and is cynical about the many 'uncles' he has had. He sneers at 'the glorious battle for socialism inside the Labour party . . .', commenting:

> We need a new form of – inner emigration. Drugs, drink, anything. I want to opt out. I don't want any part of it.

Tony is a young man without a cause, a pre-hippy, and, as in Wesker, it seems to be a woman and a mother who is sure of her cause, even though it is under strain.

As Philip, a former boyfriend of Myra's, now engaged to Rosemary, comments: '. . . Everyone's fed up with politics. It's not the time.' Even Myra comments on the change in people's sense of their political responsibilities:

> Half the people I know, people who have spent all their lives fighting and trying to change things, they've gone inside their homes, shut

50

their front doors and gone domestic and comfortable – and safe.

Domesticity is used as a retreat from the political, and this provides a springboard for personal and political conflicts and arguments. Personal relations are at stake between Myra and Tony in the passionate commitment between them to arguing with each other, the emotional buzz which they get off one another being necessary to both – an echo of the Sarah/Ronnie relationship.

Tony may have a lot of Jimmy Porter in him, but the dynamic of this play operates on Myra's territory; she is the activist with experience and a historical perspective. Tony is the outsider, the alienated youth, disillusioned with the Welfare State:

> Do you know what you've created, you and your lot? What a vision it is. A house for every family. Just imagine – two hundred million families – or is it four hundred million families? To every family a front door. Behind every front door, a family. A house full of clean, well-fed people, and not one of them ever understands one word anyone else says. Everybody a kind of wilderness surrounded by barbed wire shouting across the defences into the other wildernesses and never getting an answer back. That's socialism, I suppose it's progress. Why not? To every man his wife and two children and a chicken in the pot on Sundays. A beautiful picture – I'd die for it.
> To every man his own front door key. To each his own wilderness.

There is irony in the use of the male pronoun here, because Tony's attack is also on a family which fails to provide values for him. The embodiment of these socialist values is a woman, Myra, and he is talking about *her* wilderness.

In Act Two Tony becomes more and more childlike, 'making machine-gun noises like a small boy', in a scene where Myra has been rejoined by Sandy's mother, Milly. In the face of the two grown-up women having a conversation he behaves like a rather noisy little boy trying to get his mother's attention.

It is extraordinary to have a scene where two older women have a heartfelt conversation, talking seriously about men, but also about their own lives. They are witty, independent older women for whom sexuality is as much a current reality as is motherhood. It is the same theme Jellicoe used – that of the man who feels rejected by his mother – but employed in a very different kind of play. Here are strong and articulate older women who feel that the world's concerns impinge on their personal lives, but who test the mother/son relationship by breaking with convention in order to achieve 'independence'.

The relationship between Tony and Myra is further complicated when Tony and Milly have some sort of sexual encounter (it is referred to vaguely). This can only be an odd, displaced Oedipal experience – certainly not sex between equals. Myra finally acknowledges her unwitting devotion to her son:

> It occurs to me that for the last twenty-two years my life has been governed by yours – by your needs.

So although Tony feels neglected, in fact his mother feels her emotional life has been dominated by him. It is an anguished conflict of interests and emotions between generations, and the play ends with Tony being comforted by Rosemary, a member of his own generation. The stage direction: 'They crouch down with each other' – provides a more innocent image from the bears and squirrels at the end of *Look Back in Anger*. Where that image was full of fraught and unresolved violent sexuality, this image is non-sexual. Tony's call in the end is not for a new kind of cause for which to fight but for something quite different:

> Rosemary, listen – never in the whole history of the world have people made a battle cry out of being ordinary. Never. Supposing we all said that to the politicians – we refuse to be heroic . . . We are bored with all the noble gestures . . .

His plea is for the value of the ordinary, domestic, life in contrast to the traumatic, if exciting, world of wars and political causes, and it is the mother who believes in politics and social action. The separation between the political and the personal is carried also through Myra, who may own her house and run it, has a genuine friendship with another woman, but a shaky family base, and no currently satisfying sexual relationship.

In Lessing's *Play With A Tiger* (Royal Court, 1958) the woman/social outsider themes are brought together. The author writes in an introduction:

> Now this play is about rootless de-classed people who live in bed-sitting rooms or small flats or the cheaper hotel rooms, and such people are usually presented on the stage in a detailed squalor of realism which to my mind distracts attention from what is interesting about them.

Anna Freeman is an Australian writer with a room in Mary

Jackson's house, a bed-sitter where she sleeps and works, a rare representation onstage of a professional woman. Like Myra, she wears trousers. Although Anna does not own her home, she establishes her territorial rights through her friendship with Mary, who is similarly independent. But this female friendship, however strong and secure, exists in a world where relationships with men take up a lot of time and attention. Anna has been having an affair with Dave, a travelling American. Janet Stephens, also American, soon arrives, with conventionally feminine views:

> I believe that marriage and the family is the most rewarding career of all a woman can have . . .

Anna guesses that Janet has turned up because she is pregnant by Dave, who subsequently arrives himself, complete with crew-cut and a duffle bag. He is charming and articulate, but he argues with Anna, admitting to a fear of the 'mother figure':

> I'm not going to stand for you either – mother of the world, the great womb, the eternal conscience. I like women, but I'm going to like them my way and not according to the rules laid down by the incorporated mothers of the universe.

Towards the end of the Act the room itself fades and 'seems part of the street', and with this metamorphosis goes the control Anna has had on her own room, and by extension, her own life. It is Dave who 'externalises' Anna, taking her out of the present, back to her childhood in a semi-psychoanalytic role. When Dave considers the 'session' over, he switches on the light, returning us to the room and the present.

Interestingly, it is in the public place, i.e. the city, that the psyche comes through most strongly, perhaps because it is seen at its most visible and vulnerable; but it is also where the man controls the woman's access to her inner life. When she is displaced from her territory, the man seizes power, both materially and psychically.

Marriage and family, according to Dave are no longer adequate compensations for the alienation that accompany them now in America:

> You look at us and you see prosperity – and loneliness. Prosperity and men and women in trouble with each other. Prosperity and people wondering what life is for . . .

Anna identifies Dave's disillusion as embodied in the fear of female sexuality:

> She's that terrible woman in your comic papers – a great masculine
> broad-shouldered, narrow-hipped black-booted blonde beastess, with
> a whip in one hand and a revolver in the other. And that's why
> you're running, she's after you . . . as she's after every male
> American I've ever met. I bet you even see the Statue of Liberty
> with great black thigh-boots and a pencilled moustache – the frigid
> tyrant, the frigid goddess.

Anna contends that the war between the sexes:

> . . . is the only clean war left. It's the only war that won't destroy us
> all. That's why we are fighting it.

In these speeches there are echoes of Jimmy Porter's substitution of
the sex war for the class war, but articulated here by a woman.
Towards the end, Anna comments with a semi-ironic echo of
Sarah's comment in *Chicken Soup with Barley*, 'We must love one
another or die. Something new like that.'

The end is unresolved. Janet phones, Dave goes out, Anna is
upset, Mary comes in. Finally Anna goes towards the bed and 'the
city comes up around her . . .'

It is telling that both Dave and Anna are foreigners – here it is not
the socially marginal as in Delaney's play, but the middle-class,
English-speaking foreigners who pass comment on British society,
as if those who 'belong' are unable to see it.

In Lessing's two plays women manifest a control over their
immediate material environment (their homes) and their ideas and
work. Men are both a continuing need and a potential threat –
exemplified by Dave's control over the outside world, and the
intimacy of Anna's memory. The outcome in both plays is a
moment of suspension in which the personal/political conflicts
between the men and the women may remain unresolved, but the
women still inhabit their own spaces – physical and psychological.

Anarchy, the Family and Taboo Sexuality

Entertaining Mr Sloane and *Loot* by Joe Orton

Entertaining Mr Sloane (1964) is set in a room – an apparent return to Pinterland. Kath's first words are: 'This is my lounge', addressed to Sloane, and when he decides to take the room she is letting, her attitude becomes intimate, and she confesses she had a child once, saying: 'You'll live with us then, as one of the family?' Sloane replies, 'I never had no family of my own . . . I was brought up in an orphanage.' Here again we have two displaced people in search of a family.

Kath's relationship with Sloane fuses maternity, sexuality and possessiveness. Kath's father Kemp lives with her and she orders him around in a rather sinister way. Kemp and Sloane immediately take a dislike to each other. The language and action are brutal, Kemp lunges at Sloane with a toasting fork. When Kath bandages Sloane, she spreads a piece of silk under his bloody leg, and persuades him to take his trousers off, commenting:

> You've a skin on you like a princess . . . I like a lad with a smooth body.

She appears to be the aggressor, while Sloane receives her aggression and then takes it out on Kemp. Kath is represented as a sexual predator, tempting Sloane and then turning on him:

> You're all the same . . . have me naked on the floor if I give you a chance.

She herself confuses her maternal and sexual needs, when she teases Sloane:

> I'll be your mamma, I need to be loved. Gently. Oh, I shall be so ashamed in the morning . . . What a big heavy baby you are . . .

Kath's brother Ed arrives and tries to strike up a friendship with Sloane. Ed is homosexual, interested in physical fitness, and con-

55

tinually intersperses his conversation with comments which are hostile to women, as if he has to fend off the very idea of women in order to survive.

In Act Two Sloane is working as Ed's chauffeur, and a camaraderie has developed between them, which threatens Kath's relationship which Sloane feels is a trap: 'I need to be let out occasionally. Off the lead'. Kath is also shown as dependent on Ed allowing her to have what she wants, and there is an implication that he took away her baby.

Ed appears to be the boss as in Pinter, in spite of it initially being presented as Kath's territory, and he comments at one point: 'She's like a sow. Though she is my sister.' He tells Sloane that he had a friend and that Kath came between them:

> She got him to put her in the family way, that's what I always maintain. Nothing was the same after. Not ever. A typical story.

As in Osborne, women come between men. Ed now wants Sloane to come and live with him, and is furious when he learns that Sloane and Kath have been having a sexual relationship.

In Act Three Sloane beats up Kemp and later realises that he's killed him. In the first section, the alliance seems to be very much between Ed and Sloane with more misogynist remarks from Ed. Later the alliance switches from the male bonding (homosexual) to the family bonding, in that since both Kath and Ed want Sloane, they can blackmail him into spending six months with each of them in an inverted Persephone myth, since if Kath marries him, she cannot be asked to testify against her husband if he is accused of murder.

Sloane becomes the child (property) in this unholy semi-incestuous brother-and-sister-parent relationship, as if the presence of tabooed sexualities, mother/son, brother/sister, man/man, have themselves totally overthrown all standard familial and sexual values, but can still only be justified if they ape the semblance of a conventional family structure.

Loot was first produced in 1966, and like the previous play has only one woman in the cast. This time the broken taboos extend to the mockery of death, with the dead mother's body on stage throughout. Here too we have an alternative family. Fay, the nurse, plans to marry the bereaved McLeavy; in the beginning she is very much a dominant figure, moralising, tidying up McLeavy with a clothes brush, putting a flower in his coat, and dictating the condition of his mourning:

> A fortnight would be long enough to indicate your grief. We must keep abreast of the times.

Fay has answers to all his questions. She is depicted as sexually voracious, having had seven husbands, 'one a year on average since I was sixteen. I'm extravagant, you see.'

She is hostile to McLeavy's son, Harold, and his friend Dennis, who have stolen some money which Hal has locked in a wardrobe. Here a covert homosexual relationship further weakens an already subverted family. Hal gets the brainwave of putting the money into his mother's coffin, a risky manoeuvre further complicated by the arrival of Truscott, a policeman pretending to be from the Water Board, who provides information about Fay's murky past and the fates of her husbands.

During the course of the play Fay is continually dressing and undressing herself and other people, as if it is only the woman who may introduce overt suggestions of sexuality while such intimacies between the men must remain taboo and sub-textual. At the centre of all this is the sometimes visible figure of the dead mother in the coffin who never looks quite like the mother everyone thought they remembered. This is sick and chilling, but also poses questions about the nature of motherhood and our assumptions about it.

At the end, when Truscott forces Fay to confess that she has killed Mrs McLeavy, her irresistibility overcomes the fact that she has committed a crime and the men, including the policeman, all view her as a heroine. Fay remains triumphant and manages to maintain the façade of suburban values. She says that she and Dennis will move out when they are married: 'People will talk. We must keep up appearances.' And so, while she invokes religion, behind the lace curtains and the closed suburban doors, anarchies and hothouse sexuality smoulder in secret.

Orton goes beyond satire to imaginative subversion; he implodes the family from within, retaining a domestic setting, but countering every expected 'normal' familial relationship. In neither play is there a male authority at the head of the family, and power is wielded through the manipulation of dangerous sexuality, voracious if female, and sadistically homosexual if male. The figure of the dead mother, present throughout *Loot*, is an act of horrific imaginative courage in its combination of aesthetic shock and its defiance in showing how far the fear of maternal power can go. The sexual anarchy in Orton serves as a revelation of what might be submerged behind suburban values, as a desperate explosion of unresolved desires, and profound anxiety about the nature of the family and the dominant role of the mother.

Urban Violence

Saved by Edward Bond

From his early work Edward Bond has had a preoccupation with the nature of violence. In *Saved* (Royal Court, 1965) the image of a baby being stoned to death in its pram was seen at the time as the most shocking aspect of the play. It is interesting to see how gender affects the nature of this violence.

The play starts in the living room, to which Pam has brought Len (whom she has picked up) back. When her father Harry goes out they have sex. Len feeds her sweets until she almost chokes; already there are associations between sexuality, pleasure and violence, and the man is a welcomed aggressor. Soon Len has become the lodger, and as in Pinter and Orton we have another outsider who moves into a family situation. The relationship between Harry and Mary, Pam's parents, is not good, and Pam's life has not been particularly happy. She and Len develop a tortured affection – there is a running gag about her knitting him a jumper.

The action moves to a public space – a park. Four men draw Len into their midst, with a series of choral jokes about women and sex, with particular reference to Mary, Pam's mother. At home Mary serves food while everyone watches television silently. Upstairs Pam's baby is crying and no one takes any notice even when the baby chokes. Pam is too lazy to go and see to it, and though Len seems to express more concern for the child, he does not actually go and do anything. From his position as outsider he comments: 'Kids need proper 'omes', an indirect comment on Pam as a cruel mother who won't give her child a proper home.

Len carries echoes of Geof in *A Taste of Honey*; he looks after Pam, and tells her that she doesn't know how to look after herself. Later he also looks after the baby when Pam ignores it. When the couple argue about the baby, they call it 'it', but Len later calls the baby 'he', the only one to ascribe it any gender. In fact, Len is the only one in the play who has any caring emotions, even though he is limited in what he is able to do with these feelings.

When the men are together again in a gang, their group banter is a representation of male bonding. Their talk about women suggests that they are both bewildered and frightened by the opposite sex; they ask questions, make jokes about them but they don't really understand them, resorting to clichés.

Even in the lead-up to the stoning, Len is still the only one who cares about the baby, telling Pam that she has left the pram's brake off. Pam by this time is already having a relationship with Fred, another gang member. Initially Fred defends the baby as the others make cruel jokes. The lads are all horsing around with the pram, but it gradually becomes a weapon, until the men's social frustrations are redirected to the baby. Fred is goaded into throwing the first stone. When Pam comes back, she wheels the pram off without looking into it, a final closing statement about her heartlessness as a mother, but also preventing us from seeing her response to what has happened to the baby.

Fred is in prison, himself an almost unwilling victim. Len claims that he saw everything, but his lack of any moral sensibility made it impossible for him to do anything. Throughout this there is a strong sense that the men have to close ranks against Pam, as if the mother has to be denied; as if the baby actually gets in the way of the men's relationships with each other, because it reminds them of the presence of the woman as mother.

The rest of the play sees a further disintegration of the family. Len takes on more of the conventionally female roles, cleaning shoes, sewing buttons on his shirt and darning Mary's stockings. There is sexual byplay between Len and Mary (reminiscent of Orton) which Harry ignores, Harry here being the asexual or post-sexual husband (see Wesker's Harry). Later, Mary hits and scalds Harry with the teapot – he is continually wounded by his wife. Harry is nostalgic about the war, implying a hatred of women and domesticity:

> Most I remember the peace and quiet . . . everything still. You don't get it that quiet now.

Finally they are all back in the living room, isolated from one another, each quietly attending to their own business, the only sound Len's banging as he repairs a chair. Even at the end, when all verbal communication between the family has broken down, he still is the only one trying to create something.

The real subject matter of the play is a comparison between a particular sort of working-class family and the gang of lads in the park who represent the outside, public world of male/male relationships; the scenes in the park mirror the interpersonal violence in the living room. But in both private and public worlds the women are doubly atomised from the action. Pam and Mary have no contact with any peer groups, no women friends, so no 'gang' equivalents to the men. They also have no mother/daughter relationship of any significance and are given little stage space compared with Helen and Jo in *A Taste of Honey*.

Saved alternates public and private locations, Len acting as the device which places them in parallel. He is the outsider who moves between the two spheres, joins the gang of lads when he wants to as a man, and within the confines of the house takes on the creative aspects of nurturing, usurping both Mary and Pam.

The structural frame and emotional centre of the play is the family: its disintegration has by extension an impact on the public life of men, with the gang as a dangerous army outside. The formal state army may no longer exist, but its ideology and lifestyle are represented there in the gang's mindless violence. The moral and political questions behind such violence are of course important to men and women, but the gender-bias throughout the play diminishes the political import. Pam and Mary are respectively sexually voracious and sexually frustrated: both are inadequate mothers. In their personal roles they are castigated and theatrically they are excluded from the public action. As the core of family life, they are failures, literally reduced to silence at the end of the play. At least the gang have the ability to communicate with each other.

Len, as an almost utopian anti-hero, embodies the positive possibilities of masculinity and femininity, marginally rising above his fellow male characters, but usurping the emotional territories of the female characters. The women do not engage theatrically with the moral questions, the men literally speak for them. The overall moral message therefore has a contradictory sub-text: the demonstration that it is only men who can represent and engage in moralities. Women fail even before they start, whether on private or public territory.

Homosexuality: Metaphor and Theme

The Killing of Sister George by Frank Marcus and *Staircase* by Charles Dyer

The Killing of Sister George, by Frank Marcus (1965) is set in the living-room of a West End flat, quite a different social milieu from all the plays so far discussed. Doors lead to the bathroom and the kitchen; the dirtier sides of life are offstage. We are back in a different version of the drawing-room play:

> The furniture, an incongruous mixture of antique 1930-ish and modern, looks expensive but ill-assorted.

June and Alice, the two main characters, call each other by the nicknames of George and Childie, indicating roles within roles, and the ambiguity of this is increased as we learn that June is an actress who plays the nurse in a radio soap opera. The domestic gender roles are defined from the beginning: June smokes a cheroot and throws a doll out of her way, drinks and bangs around in a parody of the male role. Alice clears up after June, in a wifely fashion, and has dolls as substitute children.

June speaks of the way the radio serial 'stands for the traditional values of English life – common sense – tenacity – our rural heritage'. The values of George and Childie's lifestyle indirectly challenge those represented by the serial, in which June plays a major part. There is a parallel with Redl, in that an individual whose personal life goes against the conventional grain can still function impeccably at a professional level. June is a good actress, and she defends the role she plays:

> Applehurst needs a District Nurse. Who'd deliver the babies, who'd look after the old folks, I'd like to know.

The relationship between George and Childie is a turbulent one. George is jealous of Childie's relationship with her boss, and threatens to rip up one of Childie's dolls. The two also enact sexual role-play ritual after a row, with Childie pretending to eat the butt of George's cigar (the symbolism here is obvious). Despite the semi-pornographic undertones, the relationship between George and Childie is one of great vitality: the rituals are constructed, unlike those of the relative helplessness of some of Orton's characters.

The dominant ideology literally overlooks their flat – they can see Broadcasting House from their window – and it arrives in the shape of Mrs Mercy (a misnomer if there ever was one). There is a link to the war in that both George and Mercy served in the forces; the tone of their dialogue is a mixture of off-duty women's army personnel and a girls' dormitory as they make explicit:

MERCY: Oh dear, just like a dormitory feast – all this girlish banter.
GEORGE: I was captain of the hockey team and a keen disciplinarian – God help the girl I caught making me an apple pie bed.

Mercy comes to reprimand George for her 'bad' behaviour in having drinks with the boys, getting into a taxi and then having 'proceeded to assault two nuns . . .' George is told off because she has been publicly behaving like a man – colleagues know about her home life, but it is unforgivable when she goes public. Mercy and Childie meanwhile strike up a collusive relationship based on observing the conventions of feminine behaviour.

In Act Two George and Childie are again arguing, as if this is the only way they can retain the vitality of their relationship; as with Helen and Jo, we don't glimpse any moments of real affection between them. The nasty physical digs they make at one another function simultaneously as power games and protection for each other against the outside world. George hears that she is to be written out of an episode and she knows that this is the beginning of the end. There is a poignant moment when George remembers the first time she met Childie:

There was a smell of talcum powder and bath crystals – it was like an enchanted wood.

Childie's desire for an impossible motherhood is stressed in the way she behaves like a child herself, playing with dolls. But there is also a sense in which mothering is an element for both of them, even though in George's case it is difficult, performed reluctantly. Even the sado-masochistic rituals are like a form of repeated marriage ceremony which has to be reaffirmed every time they part, as if they

63

have to continually reinvent the relationship. Their need for the artifice of ritual is highlighted by the fact that the only time they seem to be in the same harmonious theatrical space is when they are themselves play-acting – as when they dress as Laurel and Hardy. Theatricality and ritual define reality for them; when they are in strong fictional roles, their personal relationship is most secure, and also at its most vulnerable. At this point, Mercy brings them the bad news that Sister George is to be written out of the serial.

At this point too, Childie confides in Mercy, playing up the sado-masochistic aspect of her relationship with George, and Mercy falls into the game, talking to a doll in a childish voice, as if both Childie and Mercy need to play at being children against the threatening adult 'male' persona of George.

June comes to terms with her fate with some ironic relief:

> George and I have parted company. And do you know, I'm glad to be free of the silly bitch . . . I am saying that my name is June. June Buckridge. I'm endeavouring to memorise it.

However, Mercy refuses to allow her to feel free, rubbing salt into the wound by talking about the other radio characters, as if emphasising George's impending absence:

> We live in a violent world, Miss Buckridge, surrounded by death and destruction. It's the policy of the BBC to face up to reality.

Mercy offers June a job, entertaining children as 'Clarabelle Cow', which is the final insult. June always seems to flip when the dividing line between fantasy and reality gets blurred, and since Mercy is deliberately blurring it, she is continually raiding June's security, both at the level of June's professional life and the way reality and fantasy co-exist uneasily in her personal life.

Although Childie appears to be an innocent, June blows her cover by revealing that she is thirty-four and had an illegitimate child when she was eighteen. The dirty linen is washed in relative public and for the first time the hermetic couple has revealed itself to someone from outside. Mercy comments on George's fate:

> Remember: Sister George was killed not because she was hated but because she was loved. . . . If you study anthropology you'll discover that in primitive societies it was always the best loved member of the community who was selected as the sacrificial victim. They felt that by killing him (*sic*) the goodness and strength of the victim would pass into them. It was both a purge and a rededication.

June's professional fate acts as an ironic comment on her personal life: as a lesbian she would be far from loved; most people would see her as a freak. In terms of the radio serial it means that her character is replaced, thus reinforcing the importance of the function of the district nurse, while in real life it will be the outsider (in this case the lesbian) who is a sacrificial victim, because the actress has transgressed in her public behaviour.

Mercy mediates between the personal and professional worlds, as well as having her own stake in the way she understands the relationship between June and Alice, by fanning the flames of June's jealousy. We are never certain of Mercy's sexual status: she is shown as feminine and a successful businesswoman, but also as someone who can play homosexual games. She is able to keep her real sexual self concealed from her colleagues but she too can only be safe if someone else is sacrificed. We are left at the end with the re-establishment of the status quo with the dangerous taboos purged. The serial continues, Alice will never grow up, spending the rest of her life prancing around in baby doll pyjamas. June plans to take the job of playing a cow, and she moos 'a heart-rending sound', since professionally that means she can continue working, though deprived of human language. Mercy will remain secure in her work, but able to step outside it into an alternative sexual role if necessary.

The overarching theme of the play is the exploration of the relationship between illusion and reality, between the real roles and the fantasies which people need in order to support them. This is enacted through the interplay between art and reality and the theme of homosexual outsider(other)ness.

The satire on the way the homely values of the radio serial conceal the ruthlessness of the power behind them, is illustrated through the threats to George and Childie's relationship. They become a metaphor for the way the unacceptable must remain 'concealed' – ie, confined to the domestic. June and Alice cannot 'come out' in public any more than George can behave like a man in public. Their relationship remains taboo, and the roles alternate between stereotypical gender-imitation in an impossible family, high-camp ritual, and theatricality. The dominant and taboo values survive separately, the second literally at the mercy of the first. However, an unusual resonance is set up in the play in the fairly full representation of the survival tactics and vulnerabilities of a lesbian couple. The power relations with regard to work are mediated by a female representative of a national institution, the BBC, and the dilemmas and the theatrical dynamic are all in the charge of the women.

Staircase by Charles Dyer (1966) is ten years on from *Look Back in Anger*. The play is set in a barber's shop, after hours: neutral territory, neither fully public nor fully private. Harry has just finished shaving Charlie, a comfortable image of one man caring for another. The dialogue is camp and intimate, and homes straight in on a discussion about sex and reproduction:

> I believe half Man's trouble is due to Nature's reproductive systems. I do . . . it should be nicer, cleaner, *prettier*. It shouldn't be so folded up and sort of underneath . . . What's wrong with having, say, a couple of antennas. Males. Females. The lot. Nothing different or sniggery. Pleasant smile; raise your hat; shake antennas; good laugh in the bargain.

The irony, poignancy and honesty of this is far removed from the tortured displacement of Jimmy Porter's bewilderment about male-gender identity. Because in the world of male homosexuality (twilight though it still is), sexual identity is seen straightforwardly for what it is, paternity enters as an issue. Charlie has been married and has a child, to the envy of Harry. Charlie is summonsed by the police for behaving, in police jargon:

> . . . in a manner likely to cause a serious breach of the peace and did parade in female attire . . . and did importune in a manner calculated to bring – depravity . . .

Charlie's defence is that he was a) married with a baby and that this makes him normal, and b) simply doing his old panto act.

The play includes overt references to the new law legalising homosexuality for consenting males over twenty-one, but Charlie comments: 'I need no laws, need no laws.' The men play on their need for fantasy; Charlie says, 'I need excitement, Harry. Haven't your guts to be ordinary, Harry. Hate being ordinary.' And there is the irony of the author's use of his own name for one of the characters:

> By hell, if ever I finish me great play I'll name the villain after meself, to prove I've a spot of faith in humanity . . . To prove I've enough humility to travel under any label . . . without shame.

Their relationship, like that between George and Childie, has to be sustained by private ritual, by ways of speaking and behaving which constitute a private replacement for a real social milieu in which they can be themselves. However, here there is no external metaphor and the camp wit is more intimate and theatrically creative than in *Sister George*, which gives a greater security to Charlie and Harry, despite the latter's sad comment: 'Trouble with our sort, you're never left with anyone.' Homosexuality is approached more confrontationally, allowing the vulnerabilities of the characters – two men who are trying to recognise each other and themselves as having a sexual identity which is socially problematical and therefore cannot be clearly defined or named with comfort – yet.

The Story So Far

Part One

Look Back in Anger centres on the identity crisis, social and sexual, of a heterosexual man. *Staircase* is a simple two-hander in which male homosexuality is presented as a relationship to be validated. The change in climate between 1956 and 1966 engendered an enormous broadening of the range of theatrical subject matter, and an increasing success in the campaign to abolish theatre censorship.

During the period a number of patterns emerge: it is clear that the theatrical dynamic (the action) is, in the majority of the plays, determined by the story needs of either the male or female characters. There are, of course, some exceptions: the Wesker trilogy, in which the dynamic of a family history moves the action, even though it has a strong central female figure; *Sport of My Mad Mother* by Ann Jellicoe, in which there is a tension between the numerical dominance of the male characters, and the theatrical power of Greta. This general gender divide correlates almost entirely with the gender of the playwright – with the exception of *The Killing of Sister George* by Frank Marcus, which has an all-female cast and dynamic.

Whether these gender choices are conscious or not, it is clear that male and female playwrights generally construct fictional stage worlds which begin and end close to home in terms of the sex of the motivating characters. There are, of course, power tensions between male and female characters in the plays, but there is always a clear bias in favour of the focus on one or the other; the action is virtually never equally motivated.

Also, the model of the conventional family informs all the plays, whatever their styles. There is the straightforward family in Wesker, the family in crisis in *Look Back*, Lessing, Bond and Delaney; the family as a structure which contains taboo relations, as in Orton, Pinter and Marcus. The image of a kind of family/community bonding pattern is also there in the armies of Arden and

A Patriot, and in the displaced, orphaned worlds of Beckett and Jellicoe.

Because of this influence, the importance of the domestic setting dominates many of the plays, but here too there is a range of approaches. Concentration only on interpersonal relations in Delaney, of the personal/political (socialist) in Wesker and Lessing. The latter plays are also interestingly ones in which women have a strong central role, and experience to some degree the conflicts which this fusion produces. Where politics engages men, even when interwoven with matters of sexuality, such as in *A Patriot*, the settings go public and (in Arden) military. The politics of sexual morality and choice appear in the displaced domestic settings of Pinter and Orton, and the wider questioning of how the individual fits (or doesn't) into the social/sexual roles expected by society, are conveyed in the everywhere/nowhere settings of Beckett and Jellicoe, and in the domestic setting of Marcus, and the in-between world of home/work in Dyer.

Because of the predominance of the family and the domestic setting, the figure of the mother assumes a complex significance, sometimes real, sometimes symbolic. She is most realistically treated by Lessing and Delaney, allowed to exert maternal and sexual power in Jellicoe (all women playwrights), feared and symbolically destroyed in *Look Back*, Orton and Pinter, and her centrality is dispensed with in the plays which deal with homosexuality – Osborne, Marcus and Dyer.

The superficially 'private' nature of the domestic setting (although we have seen that it is capable of incorporating large-scale political issues), the influence of the family model and the intense and continuing pre-occupation with the mother, that primary and most intimate of early relationships, gives rise to stage worlds where the figure of the social 'outsider' carries often the most central of comments on issues of importance to British society. Jimmy Porter is certainly no outsider, but the Jewish woman is, as are most of those peopling the worlds of Beckett, Pinter, Delaney, Jellicoe, Orton and Bond: they are either geographically displaced or socially marginal as lumpen characters, or other-worldly, surreal figures from the real world. Arden's men are central – theoretically upholders of the values of the state, but turning traitors; Lessing's characters are relatively recent settlers in Britain, or still strangers, albeit English-speaking. Finally, in the Marcus and Dyer, one of the

69

socially marginal groups comes 'inside', as it were; in Marcus in the way homosexuality is both real and symbolic (in keeping with the ambiguous representation of women by male playwrights), and in Dyer's social placing of the lives of a homosexual couple (male, and realist).

All the plays express some radical questioning of the nature of the family, of sexual relationships, and the relationship of the individual to the family as a primary identity. Throughout, from whatever perspective, there is profound uneasiness at the nature of relations between men and women, to the point where the gender-conflict affects the aesthetic dynamics of the plays themselves, as has been shown in the analyses of individual plays.

The ending of theatre censorship in theory opened up the possibilities for all these issues to be further explored. The following article by Kenneth Tynan, first published in 1965, conveys vividly the desires and needs of his contemporary theatre to establish and seize its freedoms.

INTERVAL

'The Royal Smut-Hound'

by Kenneth Tynan

For 'wind from a duck's behind', substitute 'wind from Mount Zion'.
Omit 'crap', substitute 'jazz'.
Omit 'balls of the Medici': 'testicles of the Medici' would be
   acceptable.
Delete 'postcoital', substitute 'late evening'.
For 'the Vicar's got the clappers', substitute 'the Vicar's dropped a
   clanger'.
Omit 'piss off, piss off, piss off', substitute 'shut your steaming gob'.

These staccato commands are authentic and typical extracts from
letters dispatched in recent years from the office of the Lord
Chamberlain of Great Britain, second ranking dignitary of Her
Majesty's Court. He is the official in charge of the royal household,
responsible for receiving visiting potentates and for arranging all
state ceremonies from christenings to coronations. He also appoints
the Keeper of the Royal Swans. On no account must he be confused
with the Lord *Great* Chamberlain – a lowly sixth in the dignitary
ratings – who supervises royal openings of Parliament and helps the
monarch (if the latter is male) to dress on coronation mornings.

Among the other duties of the Lord Small Chamberlain, as we
may call him in passing, is that of censoring all plays presented for
public performance in the United Kingdom; and it is this which
explains the obscene correspondence that issues from his head-
quarters in St James's Palace. On royally embossed note-paper,
producers all over the country are gravely informed that 'fart',
'tits', 'sod', 'sperm', 'arse', 'Jesus!', etc., are illicit expressions,
and that 'the Lord Chamberlain cannot accept the word "screwed"
in place of the word "shagged" '. It is something of a wonder that
no one has lodged a complaint against His Lordship for corrupting
and depraving the innocent secretaries to whom this spicy stuff is
dictated; at the very least, the Post Office might intervene to
prevent what looks to me like a flagrant misuse of the mails.

At the moment there is nothing we can do about it. The Lord

Chamberlain's role as legal censor dates back to 1737, when Sir Robert Walpole's administration – probably the most venal in British history – rushed an Act through Parliament to protect itself from criticism in the theatre. Ever since Tudor times, the Chamberlain (or his subordinate, the Master of the Revels) had been empowered by royal proclamation to regulate dramatic entertainments, but he had mainly confined his cuts to matters of heresy or sedition that might offend the monarch. It was Walpole's panicky vengefulness that gave statutory recognition and legislative force to the Chamberlain's powers, and established a Court official as the sole dictator of the British theatre. Henceforth, no new plays or additions to old ones could be staged without his approval.

This authority was toughened and extended by the Theatres Act of 1843, a repellent piece of legislation that is still in force. Under its provisions, anything previously unperformed must be submitted to 'the Malvolio of St James's Palace' (Bernard Shaw's phrase) at least a week before opening night; a reading fee of two guineas is charged, so that you pay for the privilege of being banned; licences already granted may be revoked if the Chamberlain changes his mind (or if there is a change of Chamberlain); and any theatre presenting an unlicensed work to a paying audience will be summarily closed down. His Lordship can impose a ban 'whenever he shall be of opinion that it is fitting for the Preservation of Good Manners, Decorum, or of the Public Peace'. He need give no reason for his decisions, from which there is no appeal. Since he is appointed directly by the sovereign, he is not responsible to the House of Commons. He inhabits a limbo aloof from democracy, answerable only to his own hunches. The rules by which he judges plays are nowhere defined in law; to quote Shaw again and not for the last time, 'they simply codify the present and most of the past prejudices of the class he represents'.

Since he is always recruited from the peerage, he naturally tends to forbid attacks on institutions like the Church and the Crown. He never permits plays about eminent British subjects, living or recently dead, no matter how harmless the content and despite the fact that Britain's libel laws are about the strictest on earth. Above all, he feels a paternal need to protect his flock from exposure to words or gestures relating to bodily functions below the navel and above the upper thigh. This – the bedding-*cum*-liquid-and-solid-eliminating area – is what preoccupies him most, and involves the writers and producers who have to deal with him in the largest amount of wasted time.

The normal procedure is as follows: enclosing the two-guinea fee, you submit your script, which is then read by one of three 'Examiners' – anonymous part-time workers, occasionally with some theatrical background. The Examiner passes it on with his comments to the Chamberlain's two Comptrollers – army officers in early middle-age – who add their own observations before referring it to the boss himself. Then begins the salty correspondence, which may go on for months. The Comptroller lists the required cuts and changes; the producer replies, agreeing, protesting or proposing alternatives. (A fine recent protest was penned by the director of John Osborne's *Inadmissible Evidence*: 'We find that the cutting of the words "menstrual periods" is blocking the flow of the scene'.)

If postal deadlock is reached, the next stage is a chat with the Comptroller, who usually comes on as a breezy man of the world who knows as much about four-letter words as the next man but somehow feels that the next man should be prevented from hearing them. Insane bargaining takes place: the Comptroller may permit you a 'pee' in Act One so long as you delete a 'Christ!' in Act Three. Discussing a one-line gag about the hero's mother-in-law in Osborne's *Look Back in Anger* ('She's as rough as a night in a Bombay brothel'), the Comptroller roared with laughter and said: 'That's a splendid phrase and I shall use it in the Guards' Club, but it won't do for the theatre, where people don't know one another.' If the author still declines to be slashed and rewritten by strangers, he can apply for an interview with the Chamberlain himself; but unless he has a pretty powerful management behind him, he is unlikely to get one; and it has seldom been known to do any good.

Chamberlains are rarely garrulous. Shaw said of the one who held office in his youth that he made only two recorded pronouncements: 'I am not an agricultural labourer', and 'Who is Tolstoy?' The present incumbent is more of a loose-mouth. In the spring of 1965 he gave an interview to the London *Sunday Times*, in the course of which he said: 'You'd be surprised to see the number of four-letter words and I think I can say obscenities, that are sometimes included in scripts by the most reputable people.' (He meant, of course, 'piss', 'arse' and 'shit' as well as the obvious venereal monosyllables.) 'We normally cut certain expletives, for example, "Christ" and "Jesus" ', he went on, 'which are admittedly used in common

parlance . . . but still do give offence to a great number of people.'
When asked by the interviewer which subject – sex, religion or
politics – raised the most problems, he replied that in terms of
quantity, sex was the most troublesome, although: 'I have personally found the religious ones most difficult of all.' He admitted
that, if faced with a play that satirised Christianity, 'I would start
with a bias against it'. In the six months immediately preceding this
colloquy, his office had received 441 scripts, of which sixty-three
had been returned for cutting and changing. In eighteen cases the
proposed alterations were radical. One of the latter group was John
Osborne's *A Patriot For Me*, a play factually based on the career of
a homosexual colonel in the Austro-Hungarian army who was
blackmailed into spying for the Russians and finally committed
suicide. The Chamberlain demanded the excision of five whole
scenes. The author refused; and the producers had to turn their
theatre into a private club in order to present a major new work by
one of Britain's leading dramatists.

Who is the Lord Chamberlain? As I write, he is Cameron
Fromanteel, first Baron Cobbold, educated at Eton and Cambridge, and a former Governor of the Bank of England: a cheerful,
toothy, soothing chap in his early sixties. His predecessor, who
retired in 1963, was the 11th Earl of Scarbrough, educated at Eton
and Oxford, and a former Governor of Bombay. Unlike Lord
Cobbold, he could boast first-hand experience of artistic
endeavour, having written, in 1936, *The History of the Eleventh
Hussars*.

These are the men who have exercised absolute power over
British drama for the past fourteen years. As a highly respected
director once put it: 'Why should a colonial administrator be
allowed to put fig leaves on statues? Or a banker to paint out the bits
of pictures that he doesn't like?' He is not alone in his bewilderment, which history amply supports. Around the turn of the
century, the poet Swinburne declared that the Lord Chamberlain
had exposed the English stage 'to the contempt and compassion of
civilised Europe'. To cite a few other spokesmen from the same
period:

> All I can say is that something or other – which probably is
> consciousness of the Censor – appears to deter men of letters who
> have other channels for communicating with the public, from writing
> for the stage. (Thomas Hardy)

The censorship, with its quite wanton power of suppression, has
always been one of the reasons why I haven't ventured into
playwriting. (H.G. Wells)
I am certain that a dramatic author may be shamefully hindered,
and that such a situation is intolerable; a disgrace to the tone, to the
character, of this country's civilization. (Joseph Conrad)
There is not perhaps another field so fine in the England of today
for a man or woman of letters, but all the other literary fields are
free. This one alone has a blind bull in it. (From a protest signed by
many writers, including Henry James, J.M. Barrie, Galsworthy,
Conan Doyle and Shaw)

All of which suggests that Shaw was right when he argued that the
dearth of good English plays between the early eighteenth century
and his own début in the late nineteenth was entirely due to the
existence of the Lord Chamberlain, a baleful deterrent lurking on
the threshold of creativity. After all, why should a first-rate writer
venture into a theatre where Sophocles' *Oedipus Rex* was banned?
Just before World War One, Sir Herbert Beerbohm Tree wanted to
stage this great tragedy of incest; the censor brusquely turned him
down, a decision which moved the popular playwright Henry
Arthur Jones to publish a suave letter of complaint. It read in part:

> Now, of course, if any considerable body of Englishmen are
> arranging to marry their mothers, whether by accident or design, it
> must be stopped at once. But it is not a frequent occurrence in any
> class of English society. Throughout the course of my life I have not
> met more than six men who were anxious to do it.

We know very little about the qualities the sovereign looks for
when he or she appoints a Chamberlain. According to the current
holder of the office, whose opinion may not be wholly disinterested,
they include 'wide experience, a knowledge of what is going on in
the contemporary world, and the habit of sifting advice, reaching
decisions and taking responsibility'. Of the methods employed by
the Chamberlain to select an Examiner of plays, we know nothing at
all. Shaw wrote in 1899:

> It will be inferred that no pains are spared to secure the services of
> a very highly qualified and distinguished person to wield this
> astonishing power – say the holder of a University chair of Literature
> and Dramaturgy. The inference is erroneous. You are not allowed to
> sell stamps in an English post office without previously passing an
> examination; but you may become Examiner of plays without
> necessarily knowing how to read or write.

This is not to say that a fully qualified Examiner would be an improvement. Rather the contrary: a censor with a first-rate mind, capable of penetrating the elaborate disguises under which contraband ideas are smuggled to the public, and shrewd enough to detect potential non-conformity in the foetal stage, could castrate the drama far more effectively than the present posse of numbskulls. All censors are bad, but clever ones are the worst.

In Elizabethan times and throughout the seventeenth century, when censorship was mostly carried out by the Master of the Revels, the chief qualification for the job was greed. The fee for reading a script rose during this period from five shillings to one pound, and in the 1660s a particularly corrupt Master attempted to raise his income by claiming authority over such public pleasures as cockfights, billiards and ninepins. But although the censor was grasping, he was relatively harmless; he did not see himself as the nation's moral guardian, and as long as authors refrained from advocating the overthrow of the monarchy and the established church, their freedom – especially in sexual matters – was virtually complete.

The rot that still plagues the British theatre set in with Walpole, who began to get worried in 1728, when John Gay pilloried the ruling classes with tremendous popular success in *The Beggar's Opera*. Detailed and specific attacks on Walpole's premiership followed in the plays of Henry Fielding; and the result was the crippling, muzzling Censorship Act of 1737. Thereafter Fielding gave up the theatre in favour of the novel: English literature gained the author of *Tom Jones*, but English drama lost the services of a man who might well have developed into the greatest playwright since Shakespeare.

Britain did not at first take kindly to Walpole's encroachment on freedom of speech. Lord Chesterfield argued vainly against it in a majestic and permanently valid speech to the House of Lords:

> If Poets and Players are to be restrained, let them be restrained as other Subjects are, by the known Laws of their Country; if they offend, let them be tried as every Englishman ought to be, by God and their Country. Do not let us subject them to the arbitrary Will and Pleasure of any one Man. A Power lodged in the hands of one single Man, to judge and determine, without any Limitation, without any Control or Appeal, is a sort of Power unknown to our Laws, inconsistent with our Constitution. It is a higher, a more absolute Power than we trust even to the King himself; and therefore I must think we ought not to vest any such Power in His

Majesty's Lord Chamberlain.

And Samuel Johnson wrote an essay ironically defending the censorship against a playwright who objected that the Chamberlain had banned one of his works without giving a reason:

> Is it for a Poet to demand a Licenser's reason for his proceedings? Is he not rather to acquiesce in the decision of Authority and conclude that there are reasons he cannot comprehend? Unhappy would it be for men in power were they always obliged to publish the motives of their conduct. What is power but the liberty of acting without being accountable?

Johnson went on to propose that the censor's power should be extended to the press, and that it should be made a felony for a citizen to *read* without the Chamberlain's licence.

But idiocy triumphed and swiftly entrenched itself. The nineteenth century was the censor's paradise and playground. In 1832 the Examiner of plays was quizzed by a royal commission. He said it was indecent for a dramatic hero to call his mistress an 'angel', because angels were characters in Scripture, and Scripture was 'much too sacred for the stage'. When asked why he forbade oaths like 'Damme', he replied: 'I think it is immoral and improper, to say nothing of the vulgarity of it in assemblies where high characters and females congregate.'

The same Examiner had lately banned a meek little play about Charles I, whom the British people had decapitated two centuries earlier. He realised (he said) that its intentions were harmless, 'but mischief may be unconsciously done, as a house may be set on fire by a little innocent in the nursery'. This tone of lofty condescension resounded through the rest of the century. *La Dame aux Camélias* was condemned because it might inflame the public to acts of sexual riot. A stage version of Disraeli's novel *Coningsby* was banned on the eve of its opening. 'You see,' the Chamberlain explained to the baffled adapter, 'you are writing a kind of quasi-political piece, and here you are exhibiting a sort of contrast between the manufacturing people and the lower classes. Don't you think, now, that that would be a pity?' When Henry Irving sought to appear in a poetic play about the life of Mohammed, he was tetchily informed that Queen Victoria's subjects included millions of Mohammedans who would be outraged if the Prophet were represented on stage. The Chamberlain's nervousness about holy metaphysics is notorious; as late as 1912, an extremely godly play was rejected because it contained such blasphemous lines as 'Christ comfort you' and 'The real Good Friday would be that which brought the cure for cancer'.

The arch-fiends, however, were Ibsen and Shaw – social critics who brutally exposed the hypocrisies of official morality and their destructive effect on personal relationships. Both suffered from the censor's gag. 'I have studied Ibsen's plays pretty carefully,' said the Chamberlain's Examiner in 1891, 'and all the characters appear to me morally deranged.' Two years later he ambushed Shaw by banning *Mrs Warren's Profession*; and when he died in 1895, Shaw wrote a cruel and classic obituary:

> The late Mr Piggot is declared on all hands to have been the best reader of plays we have ever had; and yet he was a walking compendium of vulgar insular prejudice. . . . He had French immorality on the brain; he had American indecency on the brain; he had the womanly woman on the brain; he had the divorce court on the brain; he had 'not before a mixed audience' on the brain; his official career in relation to the higher drama was one long folly and panic. . . . It is a frightening thing to see the great thinkers, poets and authors of modern Europe – men like Ibsen, Wagner, Tolstoy and the leaders of our own literature – delivered into the vulgar hands of such a noodle as this amiable old gentleman – this despised, incapable old official – most notoriously was.

Seventy years have passed since then, but appallingly little has changed. Less than a decade ago, the Chamberlain stamped on Arthur Miller's *A View from the Bridge* and Tennessee Williams's *Cat on a Hot Tin Roof* because he thought them tainted with homosexuality. These ludicrous bans have not been lifted, but the censor still forbids all theatrical representations of queer characters who follow their sexual leanings without being tragically punished or revealing any sense of guilt. Everything remotely anal, no matter how far removed from sensual enjoyment, is automatically prohibited. In 1964 the Royal Shakespeare Company (Patron: the Queen) put on a French surrealist play of the 1920s in which a stately Edwardian beauty, symbolising death, was required to break wind at regular intervals. The stage directions indicated that the effect could be made by a bass trombone in the wings, but this was not precise enough for the Chamberlain. He passed the script only when the director agreed to let the trombonist play the Destiny Theme from Beethoven's Fifth Symphony. This apparently made farting respectable.

John Osborne, probably the most important British dramatist

since Shaw, has naturally been singled out for the censor's special attention. His first play, an assault on McCarthyism, was presented by a provincial repertory company in 1951; it contained a scene in which one of the characters was falsely smeared as a homosexual. The Chamberlain cut the imputation of queerness and thus crippled the play. 'It's the sheer humiliation that's bad for the artist,' Osborne said to me not long ago. 'I know playwrights who almost seem to be *living* with the Lord Chamberlain – it's like an affair. There's a virgin period when you aren't aware of him, but eventually you can't avoid thinking of him while you're writing. He sits on your shoulder, like a terrible nanny.'

In 1959 Osborne wrote and directed a musical called *The World of Paul Slickey*. Before it opened on tour, the usual exchange of letters with the censor had taken place, including the following concession from Osborne's lawyer:

> My client is prepared to substitute for:
> 'Leaping from the bridal bed,
> He preferred his youthful squire instead.'
> the line:
> 'He preferred the *companionship* of his
> youthful squire instead.'

But while the show was on its way to London the Chamberlain received one or two complaints that prompted him to demand new cuts and revisions. Among several offending lines, there was a lyric that ran:

> And before I make a pass,
> I'll tell her that the sun shines out of her – face.

On this the censor's comment was curt and final. 'If the pause before "face" is retained, this couplet will be unacceptable.' Osborne sat down in fury to register a general protest:

> Your office seems intent on treating me as if I were the producer of a third-rate nude revue. What I find most bewildering is the lack of moral consistency and objectivity which seems to characterise your recent decisions – decisions which seem to be reversed and changed because of the whim of any twisted neurotic who cares to write to you and exploit his own particular sexual frustration or moral oddity. In paying attention to what is without question an infinitesimal and lunatic minority, you are doing a grave injustice not only to myself but to the general public and your own office.

I sympathise with Osborne's rage, while regretting that he let it

81

trap him into implying that special privileges should be granted to serious drama and withheld from 'third-rate nude revues'. Erotic stimulation is a perfectly legitimate function of bad art as well as good, and a censor who bans a stripper is behaving just as illiberally and indefensibly as one who eviscerates a masterpiece.

Osborne returned to the attack in 1960, when the Chamberlain blue-pencilled eighteen passages – many of them entire speeches – from his chronicle play, *Luther*, in which Albert Finney was to conquer the West End and Broadway. Osborne stated his terms in a white-hot letter to the London producer:

> I cannot agree to any of the cuts demanded, *under any circumstances*. Nor will I agree to any possible substitutions. I don't write plays to have them rewritten by someone else. I intend to make a clear unequivocal stand on this because (a) I think it is high time that someone did so, and (b) . . . the suggested cuts or alternatives would result in such damage to the psychological structure, meaning and depth of the play that the result would be a travesty. . . . I will not even contemplate any compromise . . . I am quite prepared to withdraw the play from production altogether and wait for the day when Lord Scarbrough [at that time the Lord Chamberlain] is no more. . . . I have made up my mind and, in fact, did so long ago.

This blast had its effect. For once, the censor crumpled; and *Luther* went on with only five small verbal changes, three of them involving the substitution of 'urine' or 'kidney juice' for 'piss'. Osborne wrote to the producer congratulating him on an 'astonishing victory'. His present belief, shared by most of his contemporaries in the British theatre, is that censorship is not only offensive but superfluous: the existing laws relating to libel and obscenity are already ferocious enough to warm any bigot's heart, and constitute, in themselves, quite a sizeable deterrent to freedom of speech. Would Osborne allow a Black Muslim play to be performed in a community of white supremacists? 'Yes – anything that creates energy and vitality is good for the theatre.' When I posed the ultimate question – would he permit sexual intercourse on stage? – Osborne replied: 'It might make me ill, and I'd like to know beforehand what I was in for. But I'm prepared to be exposed to it – although I might want a seat on the aisle.'

Improvisation – the utterance of words unfiltered by the authorised sin-sieve – is one of the Chamberlain's abiding hates. A few years ago, when the off-Broadway revue called *The Premise* came to London, he forbade the cast to improvise, despite the fact that at least half of the show (according to its publicity) was made up on the moment's spur. On this occasion, mindful perhaps of Anglo-American relations, he took no legal action; but in 1958 there were convictions and fines when the producers of a play entitled *You Won't Always Be on Top* enhanced the text with an unlicensed impersonation of Sir Winston Churchill opening a public lavatory.

With these anomalies in mind, consider an antic sequence of events which unfolded in April 1965. The management of an Australian revue called *Guarding the Change* was instructed by the Chamberlain, three hours before the curtain was due to rise at the New Lyric Theatre in London, that two sketches would have to be omitted. One concerned Scott of the Antarctic, who died half a century ago, and the other was a parody of a characteristically radiant royal address which ended with the words:

> Our thoughts/good wishes/carpet salesmen/aircraft carriers are on their way toward you. And so, on this beautiful morning/afternoon/evening, what is there for us to say but hello/how-do-you-do/goodbye/well done/arise, Sir Robert Menzies.

This, like the bit about Scott, was expunged on the grounds of good taste. The management at once telephoned to ask whether they could fill the gap left in their programme by reading to the audience the letter in which the Chamberlain imposed his ban. The request was refused. 'Without fear or favour,' as a wag later remarked, 'the Lord Chamberlain also banned his own letter.'

That same evening, however, the royal family themselves were rocking with laughter at an inspired Irish clown named Spike Milligan, most of whose gags are famously impromptu. To quote at length the wag cited above (Michael Frayn of *The Observer*):

> They were at the Comedy Theatre, watching *Son of Oblomov*, with Spike Milligan departing from the script to make jokes in which he mentioned their names, like 'Why does Prince Philip wear red, white and blue braces?' (Answer: 'To keep his trousers up.') . . . But the point is, what is the Lord Chamberlain going to do about Mr Milligan? Mentioning Prince Philip or his braces on the West End stage is not allowed; . . . And what will he do about the royal family? If the reporters saw correctly through their night glasses in the darkness, the whole party seem to have aided and abetted Mr Milligan by providing sensible evidence of appreciation. In other words, they are all accessories after the fact. Will the Lord Chamberlain revoke *their* licences? . . .

Mr Milligan has in his files what may well be the strangest single document in the history of theatre censorship. In 1962 he collaborated with John Antrobus on a clearly deranged but maniacally funny comedy called *The Bed-Sitting Room*. In January 1963, the joint authors received a communication from the Lord Chamberlain, from which I quote:

This Licence is issued on the understanding that the following alterations are made to the script:

ACT I

Page 1: Omit the name of the Prime Minister: no representation of his voice is allowed.

Page 16: Omit '. . . clockwork Virgin Mary made in Hong Kong, whistles the Twist.' Omit references to the Royal Family, the Queen's Christmas Message, and the Duke's shooting. . . .

Page 21: The detergent song. Omit 'You get all the dirt off the tail of your shirt.' Substitute 'You get all the dirt off the front of your shirt.'

ACT II

Page 8: The mock priest must not wear a crucifix on his snorkel. It must be immediately made clear that the book the priest handles is not the Bible.

Page 10: Omit from 'We've just consummated our marriage' to and inclusive of 'a steaming hot summer's night.'

Page 13: Omit from 'In return they are willing . . .' to and inclusive of 'the Duke of Edinburgh is a wow with Greek dishes.' Substitute 'Hark ye! Hark ye! The Day of Judgment is at hand.'

ACT III

Pages 12–13: Omit the song 'Plastic Mac Man' and substitute 'Oh you dirty young devil, how dare you presume to wet the bed when the po's in the room. I'll wallop your bum with a dirty great broom when I get up in the morning.'

Page 14: Omit 'the perversions of the rubber'. Substitute 'the kreurpels and blinges of the rubber'. Omit the chamber pot under the bed.

No argument I have yet heard in favour of dramatic censorship is strong enough to withstand the armour-plated case against it, which I can sum up in three quotations:

To purchase freedom of thought with human blood and then delegate its exercise to a censor at £400 a year is a proceeding which must make the gods laugh. (Frank Fowell and Frank Palmer, authors of *Censorship in England*, 1912)

What, then, is to be done with the Censorship? Nothing can be simpler. Abolish it, root and branch, throwing the whole legal responsibility for plays on the author and manager, precisely as the legal responsibility for a book is thrown on the author, the printer and the publisher. The managers will not like this; their present slavery is safer and easier; but it will be good for them, and good for the Drama. (Bernard Shaw, 1909)

The Stage, my Lords, and the Press are two of our Out-sentries; if we remove them – if we hoodwink them – if we throw them in Fetters – the Enemy may surprise us. Therefore I must look upon the Bill now before us as a Step, and a most necessary Step too, for introducing arbitrary Power into this Kingdom. It is a Step so necessary, that if ever any future ambitious King, or guilty Minister, should form to himself so wicked a Design, he will have reason to thank us for having done so much of the work to his Hand; but such Thanks I am convinced every one of your Lordships would blush to receive – and scorn to deserve. (Lord Chesterfield to the House of Lords, 1737)

Chesterfield was right when he carried the case against the Lord Chamberlain beyond the boundaries of dramatic art into the broader domain of civil liberties and democratic rights. The fundamental objection to censorship is not that it is exercised against artists, but that it is exercised at all.

Sixty-odd years ago, Shaw was alarmed to hear a rumour that the United States was proposing to censor the theatre. 'O my friends across the sea,' he wrote with a passion I echo today, 'remember how the censorship works in England, and DON'T.'

(1965)

Part Two

The Changing Landscape

The End of Censorship, New Politics and Imaginations

The exasperated exuberance of Kenneth Tynan's tone catches the energetic forces which were building up in theatre in the second half of the 1960s. The campaign to abolish censorship, which met success in 1968, came at the right time for the new generation which had grown up with the counter-culture of the Sixties, the pop music explosion, the various kinds of experimentation in the arts, changes of fashion, new attitudes to lifestyles and a freer sexuality. The state officially liberalised personal and sexual life through a series of Acts: on abortion and male homosexuality (1967), divorce (1969) and equal pay for women (1970). In 1969–70 the Women's Liberation Movement came into being. In an era of increased class activism, industrial action, and student unrest, there was now also a political movement with which women could identify directly and which developed a number of feminist ideologies.

The greater sexual freedoms for women through improved contraceptive methods in the 1960s were complemented by a political approach to being female which made it possible for women to demand individual and political independence. This also enabled them to make an existential separation between sexuality, parenthood and career – something which has always been possible for men. The new feminism took up one of the slogans of the student movement – that 'the personal is political' – in the assertion that there was no area of life, however intimate, that could not be understood in terms of social organisation, as opposed to mere biological necessity. Feminists were vociferous in criticism of discrimination at work and oppression in personal life, and this far-reaching critique of the negative aspects of gender difference influenced the post-1968 theatre already working in a changing climate.

The new theatre movements of this period challenged many received assumptions about theatre. There was a different attitude towards venues, with many touring groups and companies choosing

89

to perform plays in non-theatrical settings – often to audiences whom they assumed would not normally go to the theatre. Plays were constructed in more collective and collaborative ways, and the role of the writer was held up to challenge. The collaborative work between individual writers and companies was different from the ensemble work of Joan Littlewood in the 1950s and 1960s; most of the groups were run by performers rather than by artistic directors. Part of the process of democratising theatre involved many companies in devising and writing their own productions, abolishing the role of individual writer. In other situations writer and company explored ways of collaborating, where the views and imaginations of the company themselves would be reflected in the finished work. This process was of great benefit to many companies and particularly writers who would otherwise have worked in isolation. For many writers this was not just more fun, but also drew them into a consciousness-raising process from which they would otherwise have been excluded.

The general raising of the political temperature meant that all playwrights, even those who did not see themselves as 'political' or who tried to keep their distance from various political ideologies, were influenced by the public nature of the political debates and the visibility of political activism – socialist and feminist – at the end of the 1960s and the first part of the 1970s. The abolition of censorship enabled a whole new set of theatre networks to develop – in pubs, on tour, in the street, often with topical and improvised plays.

Whereas during the 1950s and 1960s it was possible to point to a small number of theatres who were encouraging new writing, there was no longer that kind of simple focus after 1968. Consequently it is not as easy to trace individual plays as landmarks in quite the same way that *Look Back in Anger* certainly was for its time.

However, the individual imaginations of writers continued to function, and while the theatrical landscape became infinitely more complex, the variety of the fringe produced a new generation of playwrights, of whom a small number were responsible for the successful plays of the 1970s – the new theatrical canon.

Mother on a Pedestal – a Doubtful Chivalry

The Mother by Bertolt Brecht

Brecht's theories of epic theatre included placing the individual in his/her social setting, as opposed to pretending that the individual somehow transcended social and material location. This conscious politicising of the form and content of plays had been influencing drama since the mid-1950s when the Berliner Ensemble began visiting Britain. However it was not until the 1970s that the full fruits of this influence were visible in British theatre, and it was Brecht's play *The Mother*, performed a number of times in the early 1970s, which became an unofficial fringe model for the process of politicisation in general, and to some degree for a different representation of woman in particular.

The play was written in the early 1930s and was based on a novel by Maxim Gorky. It was credited as a point of departure for John McGrath's *Yobbo Nowt* (1975–6) and *Strike While The Iron Is Hot* (1974), a play collectively devised and written by the Red Ladder Theatre Group.

Vlasova's first words are directed to the audience: 'I'm almost ashamed to offer my son this soup,' so that from the beginning we see a mother expressing an ambivalence about nurturing, even though she is logically upset because she can't feed him adequately on the wages that he earns. Her son rejects the soup and continues reading his book, symbolising a further undermining of the maternal role in favour of learning. She responds:

> What can I, Pelagea Vlasova, a worker's widow and a worker's mother, do?

– defining herself in relation to her dead husband and to her son, with no word for what she is in her own right.

The first two scenes of the play are in her room, on her territory, but it is clear that the son's preoccupations are the real subject. A

91

group of workers arrive to make some leaflets and at this point her son, Pavel, is happy to make use of his mother's nurturing role: 'My mother will make us some tea.' Having said that, he reveals contempt for her intelligence and her political consciousness. Vlasova's view of politics is as something that belongs to people who take her son away from her:

> . . . him running off to meetings of an evening, where things only get stirred up, instead of resting properly. All that'll do is lose him his job.

She is portrayed as a well-meaning mother, not very bright, someone for whom politics is a threat, an invasion of family life (no Sarah Kahn here). Her first political act happens almost by accident after the Commissioner comes in and smashes a mirror.

She decides to hand out political leaflets, not because she believes in any cause but to protect Pavel; she can't read and doesn't know what is in the leaflets, so her support of her son is blindly primitive. She wraps food for the factory workers in the leaflets, using the maternal nurturing role to convey political messages: the food will nurture their bellies, the leaflets will nurture their politics.

Vlasova is a *tabula rasa* upon which the play's political message is written: she is excluded from productive, paid work; she is illiterate and hostile to organised politics. She acts as the vehicle through which the audience is educated as she is given a simple lesson in capitalism and is then taught to read.

When Pavel is arrested, and Vlasova is thrown out of her flat, she is removed from her own territory, and the one personal relationship she has. She crusades: 'Communism's good for people like us.' While Pavel is away, she worries about him as a mother:

> I don't know if they're giving him enough food . . . I'm very proud of him. I'm lucky, I have a son who's needed.

When she visits him in prison their conversation is for the first time conventionally personal, and Pavel intersperses it with information to pass on to other people. The personal is here validated as a device to hide and convey political ends.

In 1912, Pavel returns from exile in Siberia, and when Vlasova doesn't serve him food, Pavel comments ironically and somewhat proudly:

> Does she look after him? No chance. Does she make him a cup of tea, does she run his bath for him? . . . Fleeing from Siberia to

Finland amid the icy blasts of the north wind, the salvos of the gendarmes in his ears, he finds no refuge where he can lay his head down except in an illegal printing shop. And his mother, instead of stroking his hair, takes the finished pages out.

In this touching exchange there is a mutual recognition between mother and son about the way politics has bound them together.

Pavel is shot crossing the border and three women offer Vlasova sympathy, bringing a bible and food. The ambiguous role of food is juxtaposed with a reactionary Christianity and the expression of sorrow. The women cry, and Vlasova ends up comforting them and not crying herself: 'You're so composed, Mrs Vlasova.' Vlasova rejects the so-called irrational in favour of a rational political commitment:

My weeping wasn't rational, but when I stopped, my stopping was rational. What Pavel did was good.

Her grief as a mother in losing her son is eclipsed by her glorious support of his political action, even to the point of his death. This is highlighted by the way she comforts the other women, as if her emotion is right, and theirs is wrong. The emotion of grief and mourning, has to be sacrificed, it seems, for the sake of political commitment.

From Pavel's death, Vlasova is ill. She is beaten by police, but still retains her political commitment, going to argue with people who are handing in copper in order to fight the war. As the women queue, she argues with them as one mother to others:

No animal would give up its young the way you have yours, without sense and understanding for a bad cause. You deserve to have the wombs torn out of you. They should dry up and you become sterile where you stand. Your sons don't need to come back to mothers like you, shooting for a bad cause. They should be shot for a bad cause. But you are the murderesses.

For Vlasova, motherhood is now entirely identified with making the right political choice, and mothers are held responsible for the wrong choices their sons make. This curious conflation of the animal/biological with the existential, lays an impossible moral burden on women, while appearing to ascribe great power to them. The consequence of reneging on this burden must then involve the echo of Lady Macbeth's call to the spirits to 'unsex' her. Bad mothers are those whose sons are wrong, and they must be punished for it by having their reproductive capacities mutilated. In addition, sexuality is entirely absent. Vlasova herself is past child-bearing and has no sexual relationship. In this context, then, the woman working surrounded by men is safe; she is not going to tempt them and she is safe from the dangers of her own sexual desires.

Vlasova's political progress has been from the most backward to the most progressive in terms of the socialist argument of the play, but she has remained static in the way she defines herself, still, at the end as 'a worker's widow and a worker's mother'. Also, she has had to annihilate the personal in two senses. One, she has been created as post- and non-sexual, and two, she has systematically annihilated for herself the emotions that we call 'personal' and which are signified by expressions of love and sorrow. The attributes of caring strength, stubbornness and loyalty which are given to motherhood are here converted into values which are put into collective political struggle, organising responsibility. She is only one half of Sarah Kahn.

Vlasova sacrifices her son and this is heroic, but the profound and painful irony of a play which does try and represent a woman as an active political figure is that she also has to sacrifice those parts of herself which are considered weak because they belong to women. She has to throw out the bathwater with the baby. Woman as metaphor for the development of political consciousness seems to be necessarily, according to this definition, at the expense of woman as real being. This means that in effect the woman functions as a metaphor for the journey a man might make to political conscious-ness, and also makes an ideological separation between the political and the personal, valuing the former as against the latter.

The mother functions as a critical emblem in Brecht's play in an ironic way, given the importance of the 'personal is political' in radical socialist ideology. The political metaphor is powerful pre-cisely because it appears to be so pure: the more the personal and female are excluded, the more 'pure' does the emblem appear. She is not-male and not-female, but appears to be abstract and mythic. While maleness is enhanced by the power of the political message, it is only so by virtue of the fact that the mother is placed high on a pedestal, used and then denied. This paradoxical representation of both politics and women introduces important questions for the post-1968 theatre.

Transitional Pioneers

Vagina Rex and the Gas Oven by Jane Arden

Rites by Maureen Duffy

The London Arts Lab was one of many venues which was host to various cultural events in film, music and mixed media, providing a social context closer to an arts centre than to a theatre. *Vagina Rex and the Gas Oven* by Jane Arden was produced here in February 1969.

The play's cast list suggests mythical archetypes – the Woman, the Man, a chorus of Furies. Like Ann Jellicoe, Arden appeals to Greek mythology as if she has to turn away from contemporary society to find metaphors for issues she cannot yet name clearly. However, Jane Arden's language throughout this fluid and fragmented play is very different from Ann Jellicoe's in one important respect: Arden reaches for a poetic polemic about the position of women which Jellicoe did not have available to her from any political movement at the time.

The play takes place in the most public and private of areas – the individual psyche of a woman situated in her feminine conditioning:

> At fifteen the alternatives presented themselves – fight – submit – or go mad . . . We have no language, the words of women have yet to be written . . . Woman's use of speech amounts to an assenting silence or an unheard shriek . . . centuries of oppression have made of us cowards and defeatists.

This polemic came from American feminist critiques of women's oppression, and parallels are made between the oppression of women and that of blacks, the sense of being colonised and needing to break out. Arden's version of the need to 'disrupt the spectacle' and shock the audience, which was influenced by the 1960s French situationists, is here translated into an approach to women's relationship to society: 'We must destroy the language.' In other words, before the public spectacle is disrupted we must have a private language which women can call their own.

The Furies are ordinary men and women:

> . . . people off the streets – those who live faceless – exposed to
> violence – the homeless who haunt the wastelands of the world –
> telling us of our lost lives.

The Furies recall the gang in *Saved*, the Fifties' and Sixties'
alienated youth, the symbol of someone in search of a territory and
an identity. The connections between the earlier generations of
plays and this new radicalism are continually asserted, while the
differences are also clear, particularly its post-censorship frankness
in both the use of polemic and sexual ritual. The most obvious
change in gender focus is that the woman is unequivocally at the
centre. The correlative to this is that the man is largely represented
as brutish and oppressive, although there is a moment of sympathy
towards him, when Man and Woman say together: 'Are we forced
to play these roles for life?'

The title of the play connects Vagina (naming the unnameable)
with Rex, the powerful masculine. It is saying that the vagina is
king, i.e. the vagina rules – and by adding the reference to genocide
(the gas oven), female sexuality is associated with power and the
fear of destruction.

The fragmented form reflects the message of the need to break
down language, sequence and narrative. The use of slide projec-
tions, music, light shows and strobe lights for the woman's madness
provides a cacophony of sensations. The violence which the
playwright sees as imposed on women is reflected in the violence of
the stage imagery inflicted on the audience. This is similar to the
'theatre of cruelty' devices used in the American Living Theatre
play *The Brig* in which the violence of the production was meant to
recreate that of a military prison, and discomfort the audience.

The negativity of feminine conditioning is demonstrated through
a satirical mock-marriage ceremony and a song about Daddy's girl
in which the singer advises her to break out of her expected role:

> Break your dollies
> burn their dresses
> and the house you keep them in

A series of Brechtian captions on a screen asks the women in the
audience polemical questions: 'Do you believe in penis envy?' 'Are
you one of the great mass of women exploited as cheap labour?'.
The woman needs to break out of her material prison as well as

away from the ideas that keep her psychically imprisoned.

The mother image appears, the male actor becoming a little boy, and a dummy ('the omnipotent mother goddess') making the male fear of female power explicit. As in Jellicoe's work the woman's roles as mother and whore are brought together, but here she is not surrounded by male characters but allowed to exert her power as a female performer in the stage space, although she is left alone at the end. While many feminist critiques are woven into the generally visceral nature of the play, its ability to make political arguments is confined by its own fragmentation, so that the woman remains at the end much as she was at the beginning, alone, with only a relationship to a (weaker) man to make any sense in her world. The play lays out the connection between the material oppression of women and the inner psychic and sexual lack of identity which they suffer, through theatrical imagery which seeks to alter our notions of stage femininity.

Rites by Maureen Duffy (Jeanetta Cochrane Theatre, 1969), has an introduction in which the author refers to Greek myth:

> There is a Peeping Tom in all of us. We should all like to be able to eavesdrop, to know how people behave, alone or in groups when they can really be themselves. By watching them we can enjoy the vicarious pleasure of their 'shameful behaviour' and the breaking of innumerable taboos . . . The Greek gods and heroes form a huge family encompassing every human emotion, every sexual combination and variation. There is no need for us to commit incest or murder, they have done it already. There is no need for us to feel guilty for homosexual or adulterous fantasies . . .

The explicit reference to myth is common to Jellicoe, Jane Arden and Duffy – three women writers. Their use of myth is not simply a psychoanalytical parade of archetypes against which to measure their views of 'human nature', but also a metaphorical way of referring to the family while imaginatively freeing women from the 'real' social family. The appeal to myth is also a way of constructing an imaginative space in which to explore a female-gendered focus. Where Arden places the female at the centre, Duffy goes further on one level, to explore the nature of gender roles in general (in a style that sometimes echoes Jellicoe's ritual), via an all-female cast and environment:

In a world of stereotypes and attitudes (men do this, women are like that, feminine reaction, masculine response) . . . all reduction of people to objects, all impositions of labels and patterns to which they must conform, all segregation can lead only to destruction.

It is a short, fluid work in a realistic setting bracketed by the Brechtian device of male stage hands building the set for us at the beginning of the play, and taking it down at the end. The territory is neutral (ie, not domestic) but female in the most intimate way: a ladies' lavatory, in which men are not allowed, and the normally private excretory functions of women are implied. The stage directions indicate that it is men who construct the world in which women perform these functions, a silent statement about women's relationship to their world.

Because this is female territory, it is full of female 'chat'. Ada puts on her make-up, Meg talks about her work – they have both different kinds of 'female' jobs. Meg has pride in her work, even if it might be dirty. And the women talk about men as sexual beings when Meg asks Ada about her last night's man:

Not bad. All right for a week night . . . No dash. I like a bit of dash of a weekend. Not much staying power either.

A double taboo is broken: it is women talking about sex, and with the men absent, and compared with other plays with active relationships between women (such as Lessing and Delaney), the tone is both frank and sinister. Often there is an edge of contempt and dependence interwoven with one another in the women's attitudes to men, a simple reversal of dialogue in other plays (ie *Saved*) in which men talk about women with that strange mixture of contempt and fear so often provoked by a sense of total dependence.

The women here are not isolated from each other and presented as individuals surrounded by men, nor are they presented in the stage world as women whose identity is totally dependent on men (something present in both Lessing's and some of Jellicoe's work). There is a cynicism about sexuality which runs throughout the play and stereotypes appear in the form of three office girls (a kind of Greek chorus) who come in chattering and giggling, again about men, in a fast and furious ritual which evokes an all-female camaraderie. Meg and Ada are also work mates despite a hierarchy with Ada as boss: 'down here what I say goes'.

Two women enter with a life-size boy doll and Meg and Ada bristle, as if its maleness is a threat to the women's territory. There is an uneasy and somewhat distasteful game in which Ada undresses him to see whether he is really a boy, with a very direct series of sexual comments:

> Well, he's life size.
> Made to measure.
> Just like my Willy.
> Mummy's big boy.
> Looks so harmless all quiet there.

A further taboo is broken: sanitary towels are used as bandages for a girl who has cut her wrists in one of the lavatories. This prompts a speech from Ada:

> Bastard men! Get a man, she says. I'll get him right where I want him. He thinks because I'm flat on my back he's got me, but I've got him; caught, clenched as if I had my teeth in him. 'Come in', I say, all soft, and I squeeze him tight, loving as a boa constrictor. And they're wild for it. They swoon and cry and die in my arms and come back for more.

It is like a triumphal female version of all the fearful sexual things of which Jimmy Porter accuses Alison. The attitude is not any kinder because it is expressed by a woman, but the changing climate means that male–female sexual antagonism can now be expressed by a woman to other women. It is as if Jane Arden's plea for women to find a language (ie, a voice) is answered in the context of Duffy's territory, where women know they will receive a sympathetic and supportive hearing.

At this point all the women, except for the girl who has cut her wrists, join together in a rather frightening ritual dance chanting about men, 'Don't need them', and when they have whipped themselves up into a fury of hatred against men:

> . . . suddenly a FIGURE appears from [cubicle] number seven and tries to get to the exit right. Head bent; it is suited and coated, short-haired and masculine.

The rest of the women fall on this figure and beat it to a bloody pulp, and only finally does one of the girls realise it is a woman. The figure is clearly that of a lesbian: the violent hatred of men spills over onto a hatred and a violence against lesbians (ie any kind of 'other' sexuality) – a display of murderous violence by the women against one of their own kind.

It is this horrifying event that gives the play the aura of a Greek tragedy or a morality play. Here the restrictive and conventionally acceptable gender roles as they are lived and played out by women are shown to have severe and destructive limitations. Crude gender hatred from whatever point of view can easily turn against anyone who departs from a conventional gender role; thus a woman who looks even a little bit like a man is seen to be an enemy. The women's solidarity, wit, resilience and control of their own territory, are shown to be a 'ghetto security', vulnerable to the prejudices they bring with them. Gendered bigotry is seen as destructive even to those who need it as self-protection.

At the end, the two women take their boy doll dummy off and we are back full circle to the beginning of the play, with Meg and Ada once again in control of their own territory.

There are some significant shifts in these two transitional plays. In Arden, the female-gender bias determines the content and dynamic, involving men; in Duffy, the dynamic is enacted entirely through relationships, actions and conflicts between women. In both plays the women are removed from the family, and the domestic setting becomes irrelevant. The imaginative emancipation of women from the kitchen sink, and the complexly antagonistic attitudes to men are tactics (conscious or not) to enable the power that women have as real social beings to be theatrically explored. In this context the mother role is marginal or absent; in Arden, Mother is one of a number of roles; in Duffy the only mother figure is passive, and has a dummy as a child. Motherhood is neither realistically nor metaphorically a woman's destiny in these two plays.

The questions raised about gender roles in Jellicoe's work are here taken further: this time they are in the charge of women who are their own subject matter. The privatised woman is brought into the public eye – the cosmos, the public lavatory – and her feelings and life-roles expressed in terms of ideas by Arden, and by the morality play in Duffy, with women enacting the theorem which is of general application to men and women.

Sex, Violence and the Psyche

A C/D C by Heathcote Williams

Lay-By by Howard Brenton, Brian Clark,
Trevor Griffiths, David Hare, Stephen Poliakoff,
Hugh Stoddart, Snoo Wilson

Occupations by Trevor Griffiths

The mixture of new hallucinatory poetic and polemic, seen in *Vagina Rex* associating women's rights with creativity, appeared also in *A C/D C* by Heathcote Williams (Royal Court, 1970), a most complex play.

It too is set everywhere and nowhere, in the cosmos and the psyche. The language is inventively energetic, a kind of techno-mediaspeak, drawing on the different sexual and technological currents which reflected the counter-culture of the 1960s, which included drugs and hallucination. The play explores the way the human brain deals with the technology it has invented. The text even has different typefaces for characters, with Sadie, the woman at the centre, in italics throughout.

The title is one of the phrases used for bi-sexuality, an introduction to the idea of sexual flexibility. Sadie is, in many senses, the equal of the men. They are all media freaks – stoned, spaced-out people testing the boundaries between sanity and madness, coherence and the wildness of an improvisatory imagination. The freeing of language is symbolic of the desire for freedom from fixed social roles. Maurice at one point comments on Perowne: 'He's a lesbian . . .' We never know what to take literally as the characters are all capable of extraordinary shifts of consciousness. Occasionally the disquisition about gender roles comes into the open:

> Do you know why women can never deliver good epigrams? It's because of the nature of the orgasm. A man's orgasm is intensive, right. And a woman's orgasm is extensive.

Gary and Melody represent the conventional male and female

roles. Melody fears Sadie and taunts her into having sex with them. Sadie rejects them:

> My vaginal walls were built in Berlin. There's no sensation there. There's no such thing as a vaginal orgasm, dig? That's a three billion year old male supremacist con . . . Well, dig this, my clitoris is a transistorised prick. Everything's tending towards greater and greater miniaturisation, right? And my clitoris is a security leak from the future . . . MY WHOLE BODY IS A COCK.

Sadie is American, a new outsider who brings the power of the new media with her. This play also allows conflict between the women, Sadie acting as a burgeoning feminist voice, furious about the power of media images:

> The thing to do is to colonise them (pointing to the wall) before they colonise you . . .

Sadie is the focus of the final section of the play. She attacks Maurice and takes on the role of liberating Perowne into a new experience through the painful process of drilling a hole (trepanning) in his head to liberate the 'third eye'. Sadie's aim is to 'get you responding to undiscovered electro-magnetic fields', and Maurice feels no pain. Perhaps Sadie's name refers to 'sadism'. In a curious way, at the end the trepanning is a birth fantasy with Sadie as psychic midwife-guru enabling Perowne to give birth to himself.

Sadie figures as a new and positively powerful concept of mind-motherhood. It is a mind- and sexually-potential motherhood, which in the vocabulary of the play gives her a significance above that of the men, while still isolating her from any communication with other women.

Lay-By (Traverse Theatre, Edinburgh, 1971) was produced by a writers' touring company called Portable Theatre, and it differs from all the other plays in this book in that it is group-authored by seven male playwrights – Howard Brenton, Brian Clark, Trevor Griffiths, David Hare, Stephen Poliakoff, Hugh Stoddart and Snoo Wilson – writers who came into prominence throughout the 1970s. The play was commissioned by the Royal Court and then turned down.

Lay-By was, according to its introduction:

> . . . inspired by a case of rape and indecent assault for which a man

was convicted, perhaps unjustly, and sentenced to eight years jail.

The play begins by giving two sides of a story, in which an eighteen-year-old hitchhiker is picked up and commits various sexual acts.

Two girls, Joy and Lesley, enact a scene in a field, almost like a soft porn movie, as they discuss having a swim. They passively pose for a photographer. Lesley comments about the event that is at the centre of the play:

> I sucked him off . . . and then the dirty bugger goes and rapes me.

The pornographer gives out 'hardcore photos of gangbang, sodomy, fellatio, to the audience', forcing them to confront their own prejudices about sexuality.

Lesley is on drugs and is casual about sex, but she claims she was forced to commit these particular acts. The point of view switches and Jack gives his account that Lesley acted willingly while Marge, Jack's friend, sat powdering her nose. There is an investigative figure called Barber who acts as devil's advocate, trying to goad Lesley into admitting that she was willing.

At the end of the play Lesley is brought in on a stretcher, unconscious as she was found in the lay-by after the rape. The scene is uncomfortably clinical. She is stripped and examined by the (male) doctor with a mixture of pornography and necrophilia; after she dies she is washed with a bucket of blood by two orderlies in white coats, who then hoist the body up as a Christ-like figure. One of the orderlies relates a parable about too many mice crammed together in a small space:

> And then it all starts to fall apart. Anarchy, chaos, total irreversible breakdown. Nothing. Void, the whole thing.

They bring on Jack's and Marge's bodies, naked, washing them in blood as well, suggesting that they and Lesley are all victims. At the end we are left with the two orderlies in white coats, male authority figures, who don't really understand what they are doing.

Apart from some brief moments, Lesley, as the 'victim' is isolated from the other woman. Marge is on Jack's side, and Lesley's friend Joy is hardly a real support. The active protagonists are all men and one way or another they all act on Lesley, either verbally or physically, lending the images an air of semi-pornography. In theory the audience is put in the role of jury – a regular feature of agitprop theatre. They are asked to accept nudity in public and judge violence in private sexual acts; they are being asked to judge the degree of the man's guilt as well as woman's responsibility or position as victim.

The play homes in on an important political question: what is the nature of rape? The conventional assumptions (i.e. the woman protesting that she didn't want it; the man contending that she did) are presented in a loaded way, suggesting only one side. Since the men control the action, it is difficult to disentangle the women's voices, and their arguments inevitably carry less weight. Either the audience already has an understanding of the feminist arguments about rape, or they will simply leave with the conventional assumption that the woman really asked for it. The image of the three victims at the end suggests an equality of responsibility between them, denying the difference between them that one side received violence while the other side meted it out. An abstract 'society' in chaos is seen to be responsible for the event, taking ethical responsibility away from individual characters.

Occupations by Trevor Griffiths (1970) takes place in a Turin hotel room, an impersonal setting dominated by a large bed in the background, where Angelica lies ill. The first image is of Polya, the maid bending over the bed to inject 'the writhing Angelica' with cocaine; the first sound is the Internationale being sung: the juxtaposition of a public expression of ideological commitment in sound backs a visual image of private agony.

Kabak is presented from the very beginning as contradictory:

> . . . dressed as he is in impeccable bourgeois style, there is something not quite right about him as though the form were somehow at war with the content.

Polya tells him about Angelica's illness: 'It's a woman's . . . thing. It's private.' When she tells him that Angelica is going to die, she cries while Kabak is 'fierce but contained'. Kabak is in Turin to see Gramsci, to discuss political unrest in the city. Many of the stage directions are substitutes as well as explanations for Kabak's inability to express personal emotions:

> There is barely a clue as to his mental state. There is a tenseness, a coldness about his movement.

The relationship between Kabak and Angelica is fraught; she carries on the pretence that she is well: 'I can't . . . love you . . . tonight . . . It's the time of the month.' Kabak talks to the sleeping

Angelica about the revolution; she screams in her sleep, and he says to her: 'No place for you, my love. No place at all.' He can only share his ideas and express fondness when she cannot hear.

Kabak meets Gramsci who briefs him on the political and industrial unrest in Turin. Polya tells Kabak that Angelica started losing blood the month he left her. Kabak wants Polya to sleep with him. She refuses because of her loyalty to Angelica. He is desperate, and honest:

> I don't want to force anything upon you. I'm lonely, I want to love somebody.

Angelica has heard and tells Polya to go ahead. Angelica lies there, a dominating emblem for the play's theme. Her womb, her centre, her capacity for motherhood, is damaged. Motherhood and female sexuality as symbol is explored in a speech in which Gramsci describes the homeland of the factory owners;

> . . . their motherland is not Italy, that fat-headed, sore-arsed sow: the motherland is Capital, sleek, dark-eyed, bright, warm, passionate Capital. Who wouldn't defend her, the young delicious whore . . .

The factory audience to whom he is speaking is assumed to be entirely male and they laugh at the joke. The imagery carries all the more weight because while the speech is going on, the incapacitated woman (the mother destroyed) is lying there.

Angelica's body is the repository for political anguish; as if she is the body politic shown when she shrieks deliriously from the bed, in the middle of a political discussion:

> It's here . . . Under the skin. It's not a part of me. It's foreign. I can feel it moving. Underneath. In the hands. In the legs.

After this Kabak explains both what is wrong with her body and what is wrong with her social origins:

> She has a cancer in her womb. A lonely fruit for a womb. We occupied the family estate in Kiev, 1918. Her husband fled. She . . . remained . . .

Angelica, like Alison in *Look Back in Anger*, is a military hostage, a conquest, a prisoner from the other side, who represents Kabak's own links to the past and to bourgeois history, and the decay of the bourgeoisie. Politics in the most publicly power-struggling way is very explicitly the subject matter, with the most powerful metaphorical and emotional image carried by the woman and by the very strength of the focus of the 'disease' being her womb, as if political disease can only be represented by the decay of motherhood.

Towards the end, Kabak has to go and Angelica, who is still very ill, pleads with him to stay. He refuses and in an agonising confrontation he brutally tells her that she is dying. He offers her Polya as substitute. After he has gone, Angelica injects herself twice and in her final delirium has a stream-of-consciousness babbling, first about the Tzar, then about the Bolshevik bread riots, and as she screams at the end, we see slides of the dead – the Tzar, Lenin, Mussolini, Hitler. Her dying screams trigger the progress of history in full view of the audience, as if the body which she represents, the rotting remnants of the bourgeoisie, enables socialism to give birth to a new kind of history.

There is no way in which one can underestimate the extraordinary potency of this stage imagery. The post-censorship freedom to represent the taboo takes the 'Alison syndrome' into both greater aesthetic effect and ideological complexity. In a play which is politically self-confident about its cause (socialism), the Countess represents the decadent past and the enemy of the future. She is, literally, decaying from within, at her most intimate core. As in *The Mother*, the very potency of motherhood as a political image destroys itself. The conflation of the female–biological and the male–political ends by reinforcing a male gender-bias which must separate motherhood and sexuality (Angelica and Polya) and must show motherhood as destroyed. Equating the reactionary bourgeoisie with a diseased womb can only work by evoking fear and disgust at associations with the private parts of women and their reproductive capacity.

The debates about ideas are entirely between men. The play's structure is simple: a series of visits from various men to Kabak. Polya services both master and mistress, both she and Angelica are movingly written, and both are excluded – literally and metaphorically – from the political dynamic. Angelica represents the emotional subtext, the play's unconscious, while Kabak represents the play's conscious political messages. The gender divide operates at both the level of the division of subject matter, and at the level of the division of metaphor and emotional significance. It is a metaphor which the woman has no part in creating; she is the passive representative of it.

*   *   *

In these five plays, the political and aesthetic shifts in post-censorship theatre are very evident. The representation of the body, breaking ideological and theatrical taboos, is there in all of them: nudity in *Vagina*, blood, sanitary towels and a pseudo-naked male in *Rites*, masturbation in *AC/DC*, nudity and rape in *Lay-By*, physical decay in *Occupations*. The same freedoms are there in the language. Such opening out in what could be imaginatively represented is reflected in the settings: there is nothing domestic in sight. Feminism's campaign to view women as more than just wives and mothers is given an imaginative correlative in the positive avoidance of the domestic setting, given the stamp of socialist approval by the way the arguments are contained in *The Mother*.

This alters the representation of sexuality, gender-bias and identity, and the relationship between the public and the private. Interestingly, it is only when freed from the domestic, and subject to the influence of feminist critiques of the family, that male/female relations really begin to be explored: via polemic in *Vagina*, the highlighting of gender-roles in *Rites*, and violent heterosexuality in *Lay-By*. The female-gender-bias is 'freed' from the involuntary biological ties of *Taste of Honey* and the manless emancipation of Lessing, to the woman's theatrical control in *Vagina* and the self-confident female rituals of *Rites*.

The mother, too, is shifting: merely a small part of the landscape in *Vagina* and *Rites*, but still very central in *AC/DC* and *Occupations*. In the former, she leads psychic rebirth, in the latter she dominates in a cluster of powerful, horrific imagery. But something new is happening in *Occupations*: unlike virtually all the male-centred plays of the 1950s and 1960s, Kabak is a man sure of a political cause. This public aspect of his manhood is not in doubt. As well as representing the decaying bourgeoisie, Angelica is also the personal life which Kabak cannot cope with emotionally. The subtext of *Occupations* is a mirror image of the subtext of *The Mother*: since Kabak cannot reconcile his political commitment with love for his wife, the personal relationship must go, indeed, must be imaginatively destroyed. And since the personal is represented by a woman, the woman must be destroyed. The threat here is not to male sexuality, but to man as a political animal, and this makes the personal the enemy of the political, setting up an unresolvable contradiction for Kabak and his socialist politics. The apparent intimacy of the bedroom is belied by the impersonal, semi-public setting in which Angelica dies.

Satire, Creativity and Annihilation

Slag and *Teeth 'n' Smiles* by David Hare

Slag by David Hare (1970) has an all-female cast – Joanne (23), Elise (26) and Ann (32). The title carries reverberations of the slag heap, i.e. the waste thrown out of a coal mine, and also the term of abuse for women. The play is set in a small girls' public school which is running down and has only seven pupils. In the common room, the women led by Joanne vow to:

> abstain from all forms and varieties of sexual intercourse . . . To keep my body intact in order to register my protest against the way our society is run by men for men whose aim is the subjugation of the female and the enslavement of the working woman . . . in order to work towards the establishment of a truly socialist society.

A vow of celibacy, feminist protest against male domination, and the desire for socialism, ring a variation on the Lysistrata theme in the interests of political ends.

Ann's aim is different – a late 1960s libertarianism:

> We will build a new sort of school where what people feel for people will be the basis of their relationship. No politics.

Elise, by contrast, is all femininity, concerned with her looks and her innate sexual magnetism. She speaks of 'the great rush of air to my legs that sucks men to me'.

The women inhabit a hermetic society, but the school is going to the dogs, parents are taking their pupils away. From the beginning we see women lose more and more control of a public institution. This is marked by the continual reference through the text to a dog which craps everywhere, and the bickering, the names the women call each other and the way they systematically try to demolish one another. Joanne in particular calls Elise the kinds of scabrous names which men might call women. She is articulate and she can be satirical about herself:

> The revolutionary consciousness – my own – admits of no limitation

to possible fields of vision . . .

For Joanne, the school represents an ideal community:

> Brackenhurst is the community of women. Nothing is pointed,
> nothing perverts . . . I'm talking about women being really women,
> being different from men.

Of the three, she is the most unattractive in conventional terms and
also the one who is most subject to fantasy, in her obsession with
cinema – she is something of a film buff. Her idea of 'women being
really women' means celibacy, and she claims that 'masturbation is
the only form of sexual expression left to the authentic woman'.
Joanne is someone whose 'feminism', confused as it is, is identified
with escapism and a fear of sexuality. In addition, whenever Joanne
expresses any of her principles for a harmonious community of
women, she is theatrically undermined. As she shouts 'liberty,
equality, sisterhood' she attacks the other two women, and Ann
and Elise continually play violent practical jokes on her.

In a series of rituals between Ann and Elise which recall those
between George and Childie, the women enact sado-masochistic
versions of male/female sexual games. In this oddly abandoned
family Ann is the mother figure, Joanne the bullying and brutal
father and Elise the vulnerable and submissive child. The 'home' is
an institution which is falling apart, an irony considering Joanne's
claims that she has 'left everything I loved' in order to find 'a
different way of life'. The world of the cinema, with which she is
obsessed, represents the world of men, the world which she claims
to have abandoned.

Joanne's hostility to sexuality and motherhood (she says she is a
virgin) are expressed in a dream about Elise, who claims to be
pregnant:

> You lay down on the table and the first animal came out. There was
> some discussion among us as to who should have the first bite, but a
> man interrupted and ate your first child which was a chicken. The
> second was a fish and I had some. You lay on the table and the wet
> animals came regularly from you. And we all ate.

Both Ann and Elise still need and yearn for men, and their
relationship with each other is an unhappy substitute. Joanne's
essential puritanism and sexual immaturity are revealed later when
Elise undresses and Joanne faints at the sight, as if nudity is more
than she can cope with. Joanne comments that she has rejected the

pleasures of the body for 'pleasures of the mind', but this is shown to be false since she has rejected the cinema for her impossible community of women.

Ann and Elise at least have some kind of relationship, whereas Joanne is atomised all the way through from friendship. Feminism is represented as non-sexual and indeed in many respects anti-sexual, as something undesirable and repulsive, to be done violence to. Women are represented, through Joanne and in the world of this disintegrating public school, as incapable of choosing art or the creations of the mind, and horrific and frustrated when they try to choose the pleasures of the body. Ann yearns for a man who is not there, Elise's pregnancy turns out to be a phantom pregnancy. At the end, her stomach is flat. Elise comments:

It's gone. There was a great wet fart and it had gone.

This is the last complete sentence spoken in the play, equating phantom motherhood with an unpleasant excretory function. Joanne begins: 'Well, then . . .', and then she is cut short by a blackout. The institutional *raison dêtre* of the women has been removed – there is no longer any school for them and each has been shown to be desiring the impossible.

The framework of the play suggests a satire on the public school system, its mores, its hermeticism and irrelevance to the modern world. Elise comments:

There was no virgin birth, there are simply declining standards in private education and that is all.

The satire is conveyed through the representation of relationships between women, and in the relationship between feminism and women, or in this case between one woman who claims to be a feminist and two who are not. In the process of unravelling the metaphors, these two objective correlatives are themselves demolished. Women are shown to be incapable of running any-thing, of having any real power, or if they do have power it is not a power which they can sustain. None of them really has any pride in her work, and feminism is shown to be muddled at best, tragic at worst, and usually somewhere in between: pathetic, brutal and abortive.

The play has an articulate, compulsive power about it, driven by the educated and sardonic language which moves fast, even when very little is actually happening on stage; the language itself constitutes the satirical dynamic. There is wit and intelligence, but there are also misplaced objects, and in the end the power of the two metaphors (feminism and women's uselessness) become the dominant subject matter of the play because the forms of attack on the metaphors conceal the object which they are meant to represent. Unlike *Sister George* in which the object (i.e. the radio serial, an illusion) is central to the plot, here there is little about male public school life. The play's energy is focused entirely on the women and the demolition of feminism. Above all, it is shown that when women try to imitate men, i.e. in running a public school, they are not only absurd but failures.

Teeth 'n' Smiles (1975), also by David Hare, is set during a night in June 1968, the watershed year. The opening image is romantic:

> ARTHUR is lying on one bench, staring. He is wearing a silver top hat and a silk suit, but the effect is oddly discreet. He is tall, thin and twenty-six.

He lies there while Inch arranges sound equipment. Someone else is doing the manual work while Arthur is visible on stage, charismatic and immaculately dressed. Gradually the cast congregates; Laura, who cooks and sews and services the pop group who have come up to play at a Cambridge May Ball, describes Maggie:

> She starts drinking at breakfast, she passes out after lunch, then she's up for supper ready for the show. Then after the show she starts drinking. At two-thirty she's out again. Morning she gets up. And drinks. She is a great professional. Never misses a show.

Laura is a 'straight guy' in this play, while all the men are allowed to be eccentric and interesting characters. Laura is a mixture of office manager, personnel manager, wardrobe mistress, she is in charge of food and helps to further the plot, servicing the characters and the art. Arthur was at Cambridge, so is in a position to present knowing sarcastic remarks about the place and to sneer at the current crop of undergraduates. He delivers a monologue about how he first met Maggie when she was sixteen, an uneducated folk singer. In Svengali fashion he made her into the extraordinary singer that she is; but their relationship has gone sour.

When Maggie first appears she shows her power through song. The songs that she sings are written by Arthur, so that through her singing she gives birth, as it were, to his voice and to his art. Even though they no longer have a relationship, he lives on in his songs, and her art would not exist without him. Maggie treats Laura badly, consistent presumably with her own ironic comment: 'I'm just one of the boys.'

She is aware of her dependence on Arthur:

> He invents me . . . The words and music are Arthur's but the pain is mine. The pain is real. The quality of the singing depends on the quality of the pain.

There is a division here between the creative mind that produces the words and music, and the emotional expression from the interpretive artist: the man provides the words to articulate the woman's emotions – i.e., the man speaks for the woman, and enables her to speak in his voice; he is intellect, she emotion. Where Arthur is immaculate and articulate in his physical and mental control, Maggie is articulate in her lack of control. On her promiscuity, she says:

> I only sleep with very stupid men . . . they never understand a word I say. That makes me trust them . . . So each one gets told a different secret, some terrible piece of my life that only they will know . . . Then the day I die, every man I've known will make for Wembley stadium. And each in turn will recount his special bit. And when they are joined, they will lighten up the sky.

Maggie is an anguished artist who uses music as a way of interpreting the pain of her own fragmentation. Saraffian, the group's manager, has the more cynical view that she drinks 'so as to stop any nasty little outbreaks of happiness among her acquaintances'. Laura makes a polemical speech which has important implications for Maggie's function:

> It's just possible anywhere, any time, to decide to be a tragic figure. It's just an absolute determination to go down. The reasons are arbitrary, it may almost be pride, just not wanting to be like everyone else. I think you can die to avoid cliché. And you can let people die to avoid cliché.

Maggie is indeed not 'like everyone else' since everyone else is male. Friendship with Laura is out of the question on the grounds of sexual competitiveness for Arthur, and Laura rationalises:

> If you really wanted rid of him you wouldn't sing his songs. And you wouldn't be afraid to tell him to his face.

Arthur and Maggie meet after a long separation offstage and we don't see or hear what happens between them. There is only one section in which they are alone on stage. There is virtually no interaction between them, denying Maggie any theatrical security as Arthur's equal.

Maggie's isolation is essential to the plot: at the end she becomes the willing scapegoat for the band, who hide all their drugs in her bag. When the police raid the place, it is she who is arrested. By this time Saraffian has fired her, so she is out on two counts. She has lost her job and her social identity, an imaginative strategy which recalls Annie in *Serjeant Musgrave's Dance*. At the point where her iconoclasm and wildness really threaten the coterie in which she is allowed a temporary place, she has to be removed from the action rather than to find resolution through it.

In this context it is as if Laura is the mother (housemother?), Arthur is the immaculate creating father and Maggie the wild and dangerous child who in the end has to be removed for her own good and the good of everyone else. Maggie accepts this fate:

> So I go to jail. Nobody is to think about me . . . Nobody is to remember. Nobody is to feel guilty. Nobody is to feel they might have done better. Remember. I'm nobody's excuse. If you love me, keep on the move.

Arthur says at the very end of the play: 'The music remains the same.'

The men retain control over their environment, whereas Maggie in the end loses control of hers. Arthur's comment, echoes Saraffian:

> Her problem is: she's frightened of being happy. And if ever it looked as if she might make it, if the clouds cleared and I, or some other man fell perfectly into place, if everyone loved her and the music came good, that's when she'd kill herself.

There is ambiguity here. Maggie appears to be the power of the uncontrollable creative spirit, but unlike Beatie, who finds her own voice, Maggie has never found hers – she sings Arthur's songs and apes the men in her behaviour. Like Angelica, Maggie represents the personal and sexual too uncomfortably, and the personal must be separated from creativity. It is Arthur, with his stylish cynicism, who survives to continue creating, even to return to a crude and old-fashioned cry of 'Where is the money and where are the girls'. The tragedy of Maggie's position is continually undermined in comparison with Arthur the charismatic commentator, a guru for

Maggie and the group, sexually attractive and always immaculate. He is never physically damaged by his environment, while Maggie has always just changed into a dress or is about to change out of one. She is physically a mess, she has to be carried round by the men, and although she certainly has a lot more energy going for her than the figure of Angelica in *Occupations*, she carries decay around with her on stage.

Certainly it is a very potent image, one which is carried through even more powerfully here by the use of rock music with Maggie as the central voice for the band's art and Arthur's message. This voice has to be destroyed for the sake of Arthur's creativity – he can watch with a writer's eye as she gradually dissipates – and for an imagination which has to destroy the creature it has created lest it get out of hand – the Frankenstein syndrome.

The man as artist is vindicated and he will have to find another woman to interpret his art. It is more of an early nineteenth-century romantic notion about the nature of creativity than something born out of 1968. The articulate satire about the privilege of the Cambridge education system is telling and effective, but it operates also as a buffer against the personal vulnerabilities of the men who appropriate women as metaphors or servants in order to survive.

In both plays there is no real personal setting: the school does not belong to the women, their 'real' homes elsewhere. The Cambridge setting is institutional and open-air.

The Taboo as Metaphor

The Romans in Britain by Howard Brenton

The Romans in Britain by Howard Brenton (National Theatre, 1980) was the subject of a court action; Mary Whitehouse sought to prove that the play was corrupting because of the way it represented a failed homosexual rape. It was one of the few instances since 1968 of an overt attempt at theatre censorship.

The first part of the play takes place in the dark, in 54 B.C., with the first line 'Where the fuck are we?'. Two Irish criminals have abandoned 'the meal, the fire, the family'. They ask a young woman slave about her family and refer to her as 'it'. Their attitude to women and sex is vile and vulgar, the rationale being that they have been:

> . . . cursed off the land of our families. Our souls taken away by the priests.

A local matriarch comes on, simply called 'Mother'. When she sees a dead body, she too refers to the violation of her family's property:

> You kill people on my family's field? You take that right away from members of my family?

The Romans are coming to take the men away: 'Manhood, womanhood, war, fury, battle fury, raise it now.' The envoys who bring the mother this news try to define the difference between themselves and the Romans:

> But the Romans are different. They are – a nation . . . A great family? No. A people? No. They are one, huge thing.

The indigenous British are represented as brutal and as vicious, and their appeal to family is an appeal to the right of power, not an appeal to personal affection or loyalty.

Three young Druids are naked, playing and fighting in the sun. Three Roman soldiers arrive and assault them with obscene references to the Druids' mothers. The Romans catch one, Marban, and one of the soldiers tries to bugger him while using obscene

116

language. The attempt at rape is not out of sexual desire, but out of a wish to conquer. The metaphor is obvious: the rape of one man by another symbolises the political rape of Britain by the Romans. The potency of the image is not just because of the shocking language, but also because in the minds of the majority of an audience, homosexuality is largely associated with 'unnatural' sex, the metaphor is working at two levels of unnaturalness.

This use of a sexually-violent metaphor works differently from a later scene in which we learn that one of the criminals has raped the slave woman. She kills him with a stone. This rape happens offstage, so that we simply see the woman's revenge and are left with an idealised heroic image.

In Part Two the action is split between Britain in 515 A.D. and Ireland in 1980. Chichester, a British officer in today's army, is waiting fearfully near the Irish border, finding comforting thoughts:

> Could see my mother – coming out of the trees now. Telling me to get my hair cut – that I'm drinking too much . . . Hard men can weep for home . . . Mummy! Mummy! Mummy! Can I have a British Army Soldier to play with at Christmas . . . If I get bumped off, ask my mother to throw my ashes on the Old Acre field . . . my mother is a stern old cow. Insist.

As the action switches back to 515 A.D. we see two daughters attacking a violent father. One of them kills him, in another act of revenge against male brutality:

> CORDA: I hated him. Ever since he lifted my skirt when I was only
> just a woman.

These sisters, like the slave woman in the earlier part of the play represent an extra struggle that has to be waged among the people, as it were, and show women's heroism representing a spirit of resistance. This is balanced by a Roman matron, Adona, disfigured by the plague, and like Angelica in *Occupations* a metaphor for the decay of the old order.

As a history play which juxtaposes the conquest of Ancient Britain by the Romans with the current rule of the British in Ireland, a simple statement is made about the brutal nature of the imperial presence, with little distinction between the brutality of the conquered and the brutality of the conquering, merely a difference of scale and degree of power. There is some strength represented through the figures of the women who fight back against their men's brutality, but given that in the context of the play as a whole the women have no political power and the ones who do are very swiftly despatched (the mother in the first Act, and Adona in the second Act), this power is minimal and temporary. Any glimmer of hope through the women is ambiguous:

> A mother of killers . . . Of children to kill the English. Children brought up right. Like stoats, like weasels, like otters.

Motherhood here is invoked in the interests of war and fighting, and this leaves the appeal to family and clan land ownership in the first Act as romantic fantasy. The violence is between men, the women emblematic of resistance and decay, and the central image relies on taboos against the representation of male sexuality. As in David Hare's play, the personal, private and familial are separated from the political overview, in order to be used as metaphor. This is matched by the excitingly fluid settings, none of which are those of an individual family. The family is an important idea, linked to matters of ownership, but it does not function as an interpersonal dynamic; just as an occasional distantly motivating element.

Existential Women

Owners and *Top Girls* by Caryl Churchill

Caryl Churchill's *Owners* (Royal Court, 1972) begins in Clegg's butcher shop, with lines that associate men with meat:

> Some nice rump steak, dear? You don't keep a man with mince.

Clegg is joined by a damaged male, Worsley, whose wrists are bandaged. They discuss power and women, and Clegg's absent wife Marion. Marion is a successful estate agent, a powerful woman:

> She's physically a very strong woman. And mentally in some respects . . . She can stand on her own two feet which is something I abominate in a woman. Added to which she has what you might call a magnetic personality.

Clegg demonstrates his hostility to Marion's independence and sexuality, by continual fantasies of murdering her. He clings to the ideal of a conventional familial relationship:

> We were taught to look up to my father. My mother literally worshipped him . . . We never made a sound.

Clegg had the ambitions of a good butcher's son:

> I was thrusting, I envisaged a chain, Clegg and Son. I was still the son at the time. I would have liked a son myself once I was the Clegg, but now I've no business I don't need a son. Having no son, I don't need a business . . . And another satisfaction of my shame is the proof that it's she who is infertile.

Marion has been in a mental hospital, where she met Worsley. Clegg resorts to consolation in the legal powers of marriage, and plunges a knife into a piece of meat, saying: 'She is legally mine and one day she will die knowing it.'

Here is a combination of imagery from the 1950s/60s and a new representation of woman: the damaged male (Worsley), the male threatened by a woman's power, and emasculated by it (Clegg), the absent powerful figure (Marion), the woman whose capacity for motherhood is destroyed and who is de-sexed. Marion later says: 'If

119

you want a girl, Clegg, I'll buy you one.' The new element is that Marion has real economic and social power, as if she has 'stolen' Clegg's gender role. Marion is not visibly physically mutilated, but she has been mentally unstable (power in a woman is unnatural?). A powerful but partly damaged woman is matched by two men, one murderous, one suicidal, both ineffective.

In the next scene Lisa, who is six months pregnant, wants to call the police because she has been burgled, but Alec, her husband, refuses. Here is a man who refuses to behave in a manly fashion, unlike Clegg and Worsley who both try to be manly and fail. Lisa, Alec, his mother and their children, are tenants in Marion's house – displaced people, more figures from the 1950s/60s. Worsley tries to bribe them to leave: Lisa is interested, Alec says he is not moving. Passivity turns out to have a power of its own.

Lisa doesn't know Marion owns the house. Lisa comments on having to shoulder all responsibility. Indeed, Lisa has to be a mother to three generations – to Alec's senile mother, to her own children, and to Alec:

> I can't start looking for a place with him like that. If I have to do one more thing I'll scream. When I think of the nights and nappies I hope this baby's never born.

Lisa enjoys her role as mother of small children. Material circumstances threaten this state of affairs, and when Lisa learns that Marion has bought the house, she turns on her: 'I always hated you, you horrible bitch, you cunt, cunt, cunt.'

Marion offers Alec and Lisa money to leave and Alec wants nothing, neither objects nor people as possessions. He is impervious to emotion, not caring whether Lisa stays or not. Marion and Alec had some past relationship which Marion remembers with some nostalgia: 'It would be you I'd call for even if I was eighty.' It is to Alec that she expounds her values:

> Everything I was taught – be clean, be quick, be top, be best, you may not succeed, Marion, but what matters is to try your hardest . . . We don't shrink from blood. Or guilt. Guilt is essential to progress . . . I work like a dog. Most women are fleas, but I'm the dog.

When Alec agrees to go without any money, Marion desires him sexually. She already has money and power. One of the few appetites she shows is for food – she eats nervously all the time.

Lisa says to Marion that she can have the baby in return for somewhere to live, and at the end of the scene Lisa has contractions while her mother-in-law makes a cup of tea – a real labour, as compared with the symbolic labour in *Sport of My Mad Mother*.

In Act Two Clegg and Worsley are being domestic: Clegg heats the bottle and looks after the baby. In this new 'family' the gender roles are reversed. Marion goes out to work and Clegg stays at home with the baby. Worsley is the distorted and increasingly damaged elder sibling. His neck is bandaged and later he gets his hand blown off. Clegg talks about having killed a man twenty years before:

> Manhood . . . some of us may think we have it when really it is someone else.

He refers to National Service, and because Clegg believes Alec has a sexual relationship with Marion, he gives Worsley poison to administer to Alec.

Lisa is now miserable and depressed, wanting her baby back. Marion is prepared to let them stay in the flat and more or less forces Lisa to sign adoption papers. Lisa comments:

> I don't see that signing a bit of paper makes him hers. He is mine. His blood and everything. His looks . . . he's yours and mine.

Lisa makes a deal with Clegg in which she has sex with him in exchange for being allowed to see the baby. Clegg says:

> On your back and underneath is where I like to see a lady, and a man on top. Right on top of the world . . . I didn't say you mustn't move at all, but just in response.

The child becomes the chief object of desire, in a latter-day Solomon struggle over which Alec finally expresses a positive desire for something. Marion is sarcastic:

> The more you want it, the more it's worth keeping . . . every one of you thinks I'll give in. Because I'm a woman, is it? I'm meant to be kind. I'm meant to understand a woman's feelings wanting her baby back. I don't. I won't. I can be as terrible as anyone.

Marion is as 'unfeminine' as Lisa is conventionally 'feminine' in their maternal desires. In the final scene, mirroring the first, Clegg is in his new butcher's shop. Worsley has burned down Alec's house, and Alec is dead, the sacrificial victim to the property values which dominate the characters' lives. Lisa gets her baby back, biological and emotional values winning out. Worsley, Clegg and Marion return to their peculiar family set-up.

Ownership is the central concept of the play, presented through a shop-window demonstration of its different forms. Worsley:

> . . . in any case the law is not for morals so much as property. The
> legal system was made by owners. A man can do what he likes with
> his own.

Legal ownership of property is unquestioned (Marion's power) but
ownership of people, emotions and ethics is different. The state can
only intervene so far in people's private lives.

The settings correspondingly shift from home (the domestic) to
public (shop), to institutional (office). In its outcomes the play
vindicates both property and emotional values, showing how
fraught the latter can become when the former become instrumental. The 'personal' is demonstrably hooked into the 'political'
(power through ownership), and the devices and metaphors are
emphasised by reversing assumed gender roles and allowing two
different women to inhabit their stage space solidly; indeed, Marion
dominates the action throughout the play. Because she is a woman,
motherhood becomes an issue, and her relationship with Lisa is one
of real conflict, unlike the patterns of Maggie/Laura and Angelica/
Polya where there is a mistress/servant relationship instead of a
theatrical dynamic. But Marion, like so many powerful (or feared to
be powerful) women in 1950s/60s drama, is literally barren; sexuality is ugly and absorbed by the ethos of ownership for all the
characters, including her. Power and the personal seem to be
incompatible, as they are for Kabak, and the powerful woman
destroys men. Lisa retrieves tenderness through her maternal love
for her baby, but we have seen that she is passive and open to
perpetual exploitation.

Caryl Churchill's *Top Girls* was produced ten years later, in 1982,
with a cast of seven women playing sixteen female characters. It
opens with a long scene in a restaurant, a public space out of time,
where Marlene is celebrating having been made Managing Director
of an employment agency. She has invited five female characters
from history and mythology, and they talk to, at and across each
other about their pasts, husbands, lovers, and the children they
have had or lost. The information is structured with great technical
adroitness and the ups and downs of their lives are enumerated and
exchanged.

Marlene drinks a toast to them all:

> We've come a long way. To our courage and the way we changed
> our lives and our extraordinary achievements.

This is despite the fact that, as we see, they have not all changed
their own lives. There is discussion about motherhood and children,
and Marlene's main function is to elicit information from her guests
although she also gets angry at the injustices the women recount.
When Griselda arrives towards the end of the scene, Marlene asks
her about the children whom her husband took away: 'But you let
him take her, you didn't struggle?' Marlene becomes upset herself
as Griselda justifies events:

> He wanted to see if I loved him enough . . . it was always easy
> because I always knew I would do what he said.

The cumulative effect of this scene is to display the individual
existential strengths and varieties of female history or mythology,
so they are presented as exceptional and extraordinary women,
even though not all had social power.

The dovetailing of the dialogue suggests a sharing of experiences,
and the interruptions give a sense of bubbling excitement, but also
suggests (depending on the nature of the production) the ways in
which the women can chatter on and on without necessarily listening to one another.

In a subsequent scene are two girls, Angie and Kit, playing in the
backyard of Marlene's sister, Joyce. There is a taboo-breaking
moment when Kit, who has got her period first, puts her hand under
her dress and brings it out with pride, blood on her finger. Joyce is
nasty when Angie won't come in in response to her call. Angie tells
Kit that she is running away to London to see her aunt whom her
mother hates so much. Angie says:

> I think I'm my aunt's child. I think my mother's really my aunt.

Joyce sees a bleak outlook for Angie: 'She'd better get married.'

In Act Two we learn from the girls in Marlene's office that a man
was in line for the job which Marlene finally got, and a female
colleague comments: 'Our Marlene's got far more balls than
Howard . . .' Balls are clearly a matter not just of biological
appertinences but the signs of power. A series of interviews with
women supply a number of attitudes to women at work, in an
agitprop style.

Angie arrives to stay with Marlene, and Howard's wife, Mrs Kay,
comes to plead with Marlene:

What's it going to do for him working for a woman? I think if it
were a man he'd get over it as something normal.

And although she appeals to Marlene, 'It's me that bears the brunt
most', Marlene will take no notice. Mrs Kay turns nasty:

You're one of these ball breakers, that's what you are. You'll end up
. . . miserable and lonely. You're not natural.

Angie envies Marlene her life. The final line in this scene is
Marlene's comment about Angie: 'She's a bit thick. She's a bit
funny . . . she's not going to make it.'

The subsequent scene is supposed to have taken place a year
earlier, so Marlene's comment above is, in fact, the last chronologi-
cal line in the play. This scene is between the sisters Marlene and
Joyce, who have made different life choices. Joyce stayed in the
country, whereas Marlene moved to London and became successful
in business. Marlene hasn't seen Angie, who is really her daughter,
since the girl was nine. Joyce retains what few links there are with
the family, seeing their mother and looking after their father's
grave.

Marlene has cut herself off from her family. Joyce is on her own,
looking after Angie. Marlene argues that Joyce could have left: 'If
you'd wanted to you could have done it.' Marlene accuses Joyce of
being jealous because she was clever. Joyce responds directly: 'I
don't know how you could leave your own child.' And Marlene
counters: 'You were quick enough to take her.' Joyce could not
have children, and so each has got what she wanted. Like Lisa and
Marion, they have each made choices.

Marlene supports Margaret Thatcher and monetarism, is greedy
for her own success, and has affairs with men. They quarrel over
politics, and Marlene asserts: 'I believe in the individual. Look at
me.' The two of them take opposing class points of view, interrupt-
ing one another, the same old family ritual repeating itself in a
mirror image of the way the dialogue in the first scene is structured,
implying that women across history constitute a kind of family of
their own.

The argument between the two sisters is not resolved; the choices
each woman has made are equal. Marlene's success is not represented as more admirable. This scene ends with Angie having a bad
dream and coming downstairs.

The play's final image is a vulnerable night-time Angie, who is a survivor in the daytime. We already know that a year later Marlene has become even more successful but no more receptive to Angie. Overall the play demonstrates that women have busy and active lives in which a whole range of existential choices can and are being made all the time. It is not a play which celebrates bourgeois success and it is not a play which campaigns for working-class loyalty to its origins. It is quite apolitical in attributing values to either one.

In close-up it illustrates this through a lively engagement between two sisters. It is in this one kinship relationship that the real emotional tensions, conflicts and interpersonal contact is shown. Motherhood is shown as one of a set of options for women, but one which, as in *Owners* can only be made if career/success is ruled out. The existential choice for women has, then, to be either to take on a private or a public role, precisely as it is for Kabak. The difference is that the private is validated here, by presenting a conflict between sisters, rather than destroyed, and the stage action presents a dynamic which places women as important beings in the world.

Owners is 1970s polemical in style, but, drawing larger political ideas into the two family settings. The powerful Marion gets what she wants and justifies it, and this is shown to be at the expense of all the men. *Top Girls* indicates different life-style choices by moving between the domestic Joyce and the business-world Marlene.

The British Left

Destiny and *Maydays* by David Edgar

David Edgar's *Destiny* (Royal Shakespeare Company, 1976) opens
in darkness with a speech from Nehru in 1947:

> A moment comes, which comes but rarely in history, when we step
> out from the old to the new, when an age ends, and when the soul of
> a nation, long oppressed, finds utterance.

At the end of World War Two a new society is promised for the
future. Three men – a soldier, Turner, a Colonel and Khera, an
Indian – come from India to Britain where the Colonel, who is now
very old (and speaks in rhyming couplets – a device to indicate an
allegiance to the past) is dying. He describes himself as 'always a
little liberal, a great conservative'.

In a drawing room young Tory Peter Crosby discusses a bye-
election, joking: 'Old Tories never die, they just get re-distributed.'
Peter's aunt, Mrs Chandler, defines the change taking place in
England:

> Once we stood for patriotism, Empire. Now it's all sharp young men,
> with coloured shirts and cockney accents reading The Economist.

The scene moves to the Labour Club where Clifton and his wife
Sandy are playing darts, an equality of action which is not borne out
in the dialogue. Sandy's role is to ask questions about politics, to
which Clifton knows the answers.

Next there is a view of the future from an old-style Conservative,
Major Rolfe:

> . . . it's not true we've lost an Empire, haven't found a role. We
> have a role. As Europe's whipping boy . . . And for those – the
> people that I come from – that is a betrayal.

Turner (in 1970) runs an antique shop with a Tory poster on the
wall, and he rejoices at 'an end to six years of Socialist misrule'. A
young man called Tony works for him. Razak, a property-owning
Pakistani with a Cockney accent, is about to turf Turner out of his

126

shop, and he speaks to the audience:

> So told him. Idea was to conceal a whole row being bought by one developer . . . But nothing he could do, and liked his face, so told him.

This effective rhetorical style excludes the personal pronoun 'I'. This represents not just the stiff-upper-lip middle class, but also the exclusion of the individual, the subjective, and the notion of psychological or individual motivation. It is as if the dramatic style operates at the expense of the personal, the subjective, and the sexual, as becomes clear later.

The play moves back to the far Right, and dissects its relationship to Conservatism:

> Beware the man – the Right Conservative, the disillusioned military man – who'd take the Socialism out of National Socialism. But also, even more, beware the man – the passionate young man who would take the National out of National Socialism.

In the scenes where the far Right is represented, the women serve tea, take messages. The women at a meeting represent the ordinary concerns of family, schools and homes. One woman, Liz, presents her reason for joining Nation Forward as, 'I want to know why to have children'. This is touching, but sounds almost trivial in the light of the important issues which all the men discuss, although Tony does at one point also say, 'I joined for Mr Turner' as an equally personal reason.

Then we are back in the Labour Club again. So far the only women who have really represented their own voices are the women of the Right, the old-fashioned Conservative Mrs Chandler. Here Sandy speaks only at the end when she asks a question: 'Lost yourself the seat?' In a following scene Peter Crosby talks to his aunt about his fear of the far Right and his understanding about how close their relationship is to old-style Conservatism. The aunt here is a foil for him to convey information to the audience, and at the end she apologises for not having been listening.

Major Rolfe shows an old-fashioned liberal sympathy for his enemies when his son is killed in Northern Ireland:

> Not thugs or lunatics, not dupes of Moscow. Ordinary men and women, sane and normal, thousands of them . . . They're everywhere. Deep, deep inside the gut.

This comment recognises that taking up a political position

touches something very deeply subjective, but it is a comment about the personal from a Conservative, not from the Left.

In Act Three we finally have a domestic setting: Bob and Sandy's living room, with Peter Crosby, who has come to offer a collaboration between the two opposing candidates. As she is introduced to him, Sandy remarks polemically:

> I do have a name, Bob. And being your wife isn't the sum total of my existence.

Until this point Sandy has simply accompanied Bob in public, asking questions. It is only now (in the domestic sphere) that we learn that she works for a community project, and is a political activist, although it is not clear whether she is meant to be a Labour Party member. Her function in this scene is as the voice of Bob's conscience:

> . . . if you don't think there are real problems in integrating large numbers of people from a totally different cultural background, then you need your head examining.

As the play ends, however, and Crosby wins the bye-election, Sandy again unites with Clifton in support of his political position.

The significant political issues and ideas are fought out by men: the rise of the new Right, an impending strike, and the contradictions of class and race. The women are silent servicers, the passive voice of personal life, or, at their apex in the persona of Sandy, the detached voice of momentary conscience. All three categories represent women more realistically than the emblematic Angelica, but, ironically, this makes them even more marginal to the 'real' politics, since they are not involved in any debate or action, nor do they provide reverberating metaphorical significance. Nor, because subjectivity/personal/sexual life are unexplored in the men, do any of the women occupy any subjective space of their own. The political is seen to happen between men, while the personal is merely referred to by the presence of women. The two spheres are held separate.

Maydays by David Edgar (1983, Royal Shakespeare Company) also opens in 1945. It is May Day, with the Internationale sung 'beautifully – by working class English voices'. Jeremy Crowther, aged seventeen, a member of the Young Communist League, is celebrating the victory for socialism and a Labour government, in a speech delivered directly to the audience.

We then move on to 1956 and the Hungarian uprising where Lermontov and a female stenographer represent the Russian army trying to put down the rebellion. Lermontov lets a young man escape; the man is shot in a burst of gunfire offstage and we are left with the ambiguity of not knowing whether it was a deliberately cruel act or whether it was a gesture of personal generosity which Lermontov himself must have known to be futile.

We return to Crowther in 1962, now a schoolmaster at a minor public school. Seventeen-year-old Martin Glass, a young rebel, wears a CND badge. Jeremy comments on the symbol of CND, 'the circle you see represents the unborn child . . .' Martin's father was a vicar: 'He's got a bit of a private income, but it's been considerably eroded over recent years.' His mother is 'a very proper woman'.

Martin and Jeremy strike a chord of sympathy over CND, Jeremy remembering his radical past. Martin comments:

> Then I imagine you'd resent as much as I do the idea you want to ban the bomb because you want to kill your mother.

In this moment of friendship, after which Crowther gives him a cigarette, the two men dismiss any crude psychological interpretation of political motives, and also imply rejection of the personal, in a collusion between men. Jeremy left the Party over Hungary, and he comments in recollection of those who struggled in the 1930s:

> And what we'd missed, of course, was all the glory. And indeed the confidence that once you'd cracked the shackles of the system, every man indeed would be an Aristotle or a Michelangelo. Because in a way, it had already happened. And it hadn't turned out how we thought it would at all. Oh, it was decent, sure, and reasonably caring in its bureaucratic way . . . But you realise there's something missing. The working class is freer than it's ever been . . . But somewhere . . . You hear a kind of scream. The scream of the possessed. And you realise there's all the difference in the world between liberty and liberation.

Despite its cynical sadness, these are the sentiments that the playwright generation of the mid-1950s and the early 1960s were exploring. There are hints of the needs of Ronnie (Wesker) and Tony (Lessing). Martin's youthful idealism counterpoints Crowther; where Jeremy looks to the past, Martin looks to the future.

Martin is in California in 1967 with the hippies and the draft resisters. An American woman called Cathy provides exposition for Martin and the audience. In May 1968 Martin is very much in the thick of British student protest, living in a Midlands commune where in the living room there is a washing line with nappies, and a man stencilling: politics at work at home as well as out on the streets.

Amanda comes in carrying a tray of dirty mugs. She banters with Martin about a conference she was unable to go to because she was looking after the children. James Grain tries to draw Martin into membership of the Socialist Vanguard, an ultra-left organisation which includes as part of its programme support for Vietnam and has the slogan 'the revolution is the festival of the oppressed'. Amanda's throwaway comment, 'Well, I suppose – it's only rock and roll' is an ironic, part-dismissive, part-affectionate, comment on the stage of history through which they are all passing. James appeals against the psychological in Martin:

> I frankly couldn't give a toss about your guilty conscience, I don't even care if you're repressing latent homosexuality, or if you really want to kill your mother . . . until you sacrifice your individual conscience, then you will be frankly useless to the building of a party.

Amanda agrees with this. When she and James are alone she says directly: 'Let's go and fuck, okay?' Sexuality appears as a functional activity and certainly not one that arouses the same passions as ideas. The individual and personal have to be thrown aside if political commitment is to be embraced.

In Moscow Lermontov is changing his ideas. Originally he thought Hungary was a mistake, but now he believes it was right and is trying to get other people to sign his petition. He believes in ideals but not in brutal practices. Back in London there is a student occupation at Leeds University where Jeremy is teaching. Jeremy's comment is ironic: 'I fought for this, I fought for you.' But he cannot support their action. In 1970, during the invasion of Cambodia, Martin joins Socialist Vanguard: 'I want to be a traitor to my class.' Amanda gets a membership card for him, implying that she has more access to the party.

The personal is subsumed into the political for Martin. In 1972 Martin visits Jeremy:

JEREMY: Oh, is there a Mrs Glass?

MARTIN: The Party.

One of the debates running through the play is the distinction, if any, between a subjective and an objective position. James comments about another member of the group:

> He may think he is a revolutionary. Objectively he is nothing of the kind.

And he comments to Martin that he 'couldn't care less what you feel, it's what you think and do'. Martin is expelled from the party for not thinking or doing the correct things, and for apparently feeling things that are in conflict with his political allegiance.

Amanda has already left the party in 1974, when she appears carrying glasses and a bottle of Scotch. Martin's comment: 'You jumped, I was pushed,' does not enlighten us as to why she left (or why she joined). Amanda again comments that she is on child-minding duty, and their exchange about sex is a little more subtle than the exchange between her and James, although still fairly impersonal, Amanda quoting from a Beatles' song, 'She's Leaving Home'.

At one point Amanda begins to venture into the emotional sphere when she starts saying, 'Martin, I used to cry – ', but a group of friends rush in, so that any emotion is blocked. Later Martin refers to Amanda's daughter who used to mind her going to meetings, but the mood of the moment has gone and Amanda answers unemotionally.

Despite her continually changing position, Amanda is never given the chance to voice doubts, crises of conscience, or contradictions; she is simply a creature of the ideological moment. Amanda is a real mother, and she also 'looks after' Martin ideologically.

Martin and Amanda live together and arrive at a party at the end of the Vietnam war in 1975, Martin going through yet another crisis of conscience. Amanda is the strong, reassuring one. She calls him 'lovey', but does not enter into any emotional engagement either with or against him, until she bursts out:

> Martin, I'm not sure that I'm presently that interested in what you think . . . Or what you feel . . . the problem does come down to what you are . . . try to imagine what life would be like if you didn't have a cock. I think that would be really helpful. Actually.

The remark comes out of the blue, like Sandy's proto-feminist comment in the previous play. It has no dramatic context since there has been no conflict over gender between Martin and Amanda, and no feminist presence in any form of power base through the play in the way that the socialist power bases are very carefully distinguished from one another and allowed to come into conflict. Women do not relate to other women, only to the men.

Martin self-consciously sees himself as part of history:

> And as once again the proofs pile up that we are catastrophically wrong, we change the question . . . that all the stillbirths, all the monstrous misbegottens with no legs or stomachs but with all those twitching ears and beady little eyes, that they're the deviation and that *therefore* somewhere in the future there must be a norm.

The desire for an ideal reminds us of Jimmy Porter in an image of failed ideals. The image, as we will note, is of distorted births which carry reverberations from some of the imagery of *Slag* and *Occupations*. At the end Amanda dismissively and a little ironically repeats her catchphrase, '. . . it's only rock and roll', implying yet again that what is important is the moment, not the longer historical perspective. She floats through history on whatever tide, whereas at least Martin struggles. At the end of the 1970s, Amanda is at an anti-Nazi League rock festival – if it moves, Amanda supports it because it's only rock and roll.

The Amanda/Martin relationship is illuminated in a conversation with James. She tells him about the time she tried to explain to Martin why she used to cry:

> All those opportunities, those bold bright schools and gleaming universities. That our folks had never had themselves, but had been through a slump and then a war to win for us. And if we didn't finish it, if we didn't get it right this time, if we didn't actually complete the building of the New Jerusalem, for them, for us, then what the fuck were we about?
> And I left your party when I realised the one absolute condition of my membership was checking in those feelings at the door.

The reference to 'feelings' when measured against Amanda's actions, means simply doing what you want without thought. Amanda's final comment is another pop reference: 'For me it all went off with Elton John.' In a sense Amanda functions as the chorus – not because she sings songs, but because of her references to them; the lyrics of popular music are the ones that carry the commentary on the rest of the action, and not on her own life.

The introduction of convincing personal motivation comes when Lermontov, who has been imprisoned as a dissident, encounters the woman stenographer from the first scene who betrayed him. Clara, the stenographer, says she did it because he sneered at her for being an ignorant peasant girl. He comments:

> But what was visited on me broke all the rules . . . That wasn't faceless. It was sharp and real and *personal*.

In an imaginative moment that recalls the outsider figures of the 1950s/60s, it is the foreigners, the strangers, between whom the really personal gestures take place. It is not just an illustration that people in the Soviet Union can act out of personal motivation, but it is a displacement of subjective personal motivation from the British political arena to a different one, and in a small way echoes the way the 50s and 60s plays made use of the 'outsider' figure to comment on British society.

At the end, Martin travels, if not quite a full circle, then certainly back to something like his parents' views, and ends up working for a Tory think-tank. When he encounters Amanda and she is on to the next thing, he jokes:

> So what's your present bag then? Apart, that is, from battered lesbians against the bomb.

Amanda makes a propaganda point about missiles, and by sheer coincidence (!) Martin actually lives near an American air-force base in his father's house which he has just bought back. Amanda defends the anti-organisation line of the anti-nuclear women:

> But I think in fact that in the end they are doing, what we all are trying to do, in our many different ways, can only be accounted for by something in the nature of our species which resents, rejects and ultimately will resist a world that is demonstrably and in this case dramatically wrong and mad and unjust and unfair.

The play ends with Martin and Amanda at a demonstration outside the American air-force base in which the hardware, the guns, the loudspeaker, the sirens, the searchlights and the wire, the big government paraphernalia, are contrasted with the vulnerability of unarmed female bodies in protest.

Politics is presented in two strands in the play. There are the sets of political arguments through which Martin moves and in relation to which he struggles all the time; the dynamic of the action follows his story. Then there is the off-centre character of Amanda who never engages intellectually with any issue. In the speech quoted earlier she appeals to a biologistic argument 'in the nature of our species', for the vitality of political protest. Amanda is one political move ahead of Martin, which gives her an apparent importance in 'leading' his politics. Yet she does so without debate, 'instinctively', as it were, giving her an overwhelmingly important metaphorical significance. This may look as if it is a chivalric image of the power of women to lead change, but it is a power with no social base. It happens without conscious control, so that rebellion itself becomes an infantile disorder, the correlative being that when rebels grow up they have to leave idealism behind (i.e. as Martin does and as Jeremy did during his time). At the end of the play Amanda's daughter carries on the torch: 'it's only rock and roll'. This must imply that women do not grow up, since women continue to carry the innocent message of protest.

Of these two approaches to politics, the intellectual/conceptual is given greater value. The world of politics 'belongs' to the men, and women are not given any politics, even on the left. Feminism is fleetingly referred to, but it is not part of the visible fabric of Amanda's life. Indeed, women again have to be excluded from real politics in order to carry the emotional subjective and childlike torch of hope. The potency of this play, with its vigorous intellectual demands, shows the way ideas impinge on people's lives, but works by denying its characters, male and female, space for emotional/ sexual entanglements, with a vision of heroism in which men monopolise politics and the women service or symbolise the continuity of hope and the paradoxical vanity of such protest to affect or change anything.

Institutional Power and Male Sexuality

Operation Bad Apple by G. F. Newman

Tibetan Inroads by Stephen Lowe

Bent by Martin Sherman

Operation Bad Apple (Royal Court, 1982) is about Metropolitan Police Force corruption and has an all-male cast. The play is a mixture of old-fashioned morality and new-style agitprop. It opens in the latter style with Assistant Commissioner Vyvyan making a speech to a group of detectives (the audience) from the country who are to investigate corruption in the Metropolitan force:

> What we're talking about here is the odd bad apple in an otherwise sound barrel . . . so let us dig it out.

The play is structured like a thriller with the guilty and the innocent all of the same ilk; the real dynamic lies in the slow exposure of power relations within the police force.

There are a number of conflicts and intrigues. The first conflict is between town and country police. Vyvyan calls the rural police the 'turnip squad'. Detective Chief Inspector Terry Sneed delivers money to Vyvyan in his Esher house, during which Vyvyan's philosophy is spelled out:

> Greed I can tolerate . . . I'm a firm believer in the government's monetarist policy, letting the market find its own price – what is unforgivable is carelessness.

Sneed is angry at the way Operation Bad Apple is going:

> They're bringing more and more policemen on to Operation Bad Apple to interview more and more policemen. For what? A big fat fuck all at the end of the day.

This swearing has an emotional significance in an all-male play where sexual terminology appears in outbursts whenever any

135

character, whatever his rank, is at bay. When two rural police
officers interview a Metropolitan officer about corruption, his
response is: 'This is fucking outrageous, you cunts.' The juxtaposition of reference to sexual intercourse with reference to female
genitalia is a motif throughout the play and this combination of
disgusts occurs at points where the power the men have, however
small, is about to be taken away. Institutional power, when it is
being damaged, is metaphorically represented through emotions of
disgust which are only gender-specific in reference to women. When
Feast, one of the corrupt policemen, is asked what he is going to do,
he says, 'To be perfectly honest, sir, I'm fucked if I know.'

As the nets begin to close in on Sneed, Vyvyan becomes worried.
Sneed is arrested, the sure-footed corrupt policeman now being
treated like a villain but never losing his sense of self-confidence. He
has a great sense of self-irony: 'It's like sitting here listening to
myself.' Disgust at homosexuality recalls the imagery in *Romans*
when Sneed says:

> I've known some of the hardest villains who'd have let me fuck them
> up the arse for a bit of help.

Success in power promises sexuality, as Sneed says:

> I suppose it gives you a hard on, does it, nicking other policemen?

Anyone not on Sneed's side is automatically 'a cunt'.

The morality motif works similarly to that in *Sister George* and *A
Patriot*. In all three an individual becomes the scapegoat in order to
maintain the status quo. Commander Wiseman, the man at the top,
makes this explicit to Sneed:

> This is not something you should take personally. You're simply a
> victim of the excess need to re-establish some sense of balance.

But Sneed still has power in the form of detailed information
about other corrupt policemen. By the end of the scene, Commander Wiseman is uncomfortable that the net is getting too close:
'These country detectives are trying a little too hard.' The whole
scene is overheard by policemen who are bugging the cell.

At the same time as the police are trying to put their own house in
order, their image to the public has to be justified. Sneed reckons
that ninety-five per cent of the CID are corrupt:

> I mean, let's face it, everyone's at it nowadays. 'S a fact of life.

When Vyvyan is confronted with information about him, he not only takes up the language ('Well, you realise it's all fucking nonsense, don't you'), but also gets the shits and has to go off and sit in the lavatory. The Director of Public Prosecutions says they must find a psychiatrist to see Sneed, and here too Sneed effects a reversal, ending with a collusive chat about boat-mooring fees.

By the end there are a number of scapegoats, but Sneed is not among them. He holds too many strings of power within the machine to be simply dispensable as a scapegoat, and the play closes with Sneed making a speech to the detectives (i.e. the audience):

Three bad apples – even in a barrel as vast as the Met is a lot . . .
you've worked long hard hours and have been away from your wives
and families for longer than is sometimes good.

The moral is that the structure of the institution has been vindicated and will carry on as before. In terms of gender analysis the representation of power relations in the police force is literally between men. The play examines the structure of power from within by showing the intricacies with which institutional power, private corruption and personal/sexual fear, are continually intertwined. It displaces its emotions onto women only in its use of language. When the men discuss women, or sexual relations with women, they are brutal, misogynist, and contemptuous, except about their wives. They still have a good, solid, old-fashioned double standard loyalty to their families alongside their immorality. They remark that being so far away from home for so long doesn't do 'anyone's family life much good'. At the same time they talk quite cynically about women they have picked up in town: 'I must have screwed more women than I knew existed in Wiltshire.' Sneed has an unhappy personal life and is promiscuous. The meaning of sexuality and associations with women in their own psyches are tied to social power to give the men a personal and a political identity, which operates all the more powerfully because it has to be expressed through male/male relations; there are no women characters upon whom to displace the personal, or to carry the metaphors for men's consciences. This means, however, that there are no familial or personal relationships in the play, only those based on power, and the settings, outdoor, or police station, reinforce this.

Tibetan Inroads by Stephen Lowe (Royal Court, 1981) has a mixed cast and is set in Tibet. The language is poetic and gentle. It begins with a love scene between Dorja, a young Tibetan man, and Genyen, a young woman married to a much older landowner, Jamyang. Dorja is both butcher and blacksmith, someone who nurtures people, provides meat and hardware for them. The love scene between him and Genyen is delicate, the two dress each other at the end and Genyen builds a stone shrine to love. Intercut with this is a scene in which monks renounce everything material, juxtaposing the abdication of all that is material with the celebration of illicit heterosexual love.

At home Dorja's mother, the head of the household, goes on at him about getting married:

I'm talking business. It's my business as well. We need a woman.

This mother is in control of her sons and also *au fait* with what goes on elsewhere:

Nothing happens behind those walls that an old woman can't understand.

The feudal family here is a self-sufficient economic unit (cf *Romans in Britain*), and its relations not merely voluntary. Dorja is therefore presented as either a son to his mother or potential husband – i.e. in terms of his relationship to women, a reversal of the expected. Tashi, Dorja's Buddhist monk brother, comes to arrest him. Dorja has to put on chains and publicly walk up the hill to the monastery. Tashi places duty above family loyalty:

I have been sent to understand my duty. It's a test for me, and if I fail, I fail you and all my teachers.

When Dorja is tried by Genyen's husband for 'stealing my wife in adultery' he loses the power of speech and can only mumble Genyen's name. The loss of speech here foreshadows his sentence. The abbot is critical of the fact that he has acted out his sexual desires:

You need to be free of those desires that torment you. The judgement: all that he earns to be confiscated to Jamyang and the prisoner himself to be emasculated . . . You are to be castrated.

Dorja is deprived of his property and his sexual powers as a punishment for having 'stolen' another man's wife. When he is recovering and delirious, he equates death with lack of sexual powers: 'Why am I not dead? You took life from me.' His brother's version is:

> We have lifted the rock. You are free of it. The traces of desire that
> still haunt you will soon fade away.

His mother is given to Jamyang, as a servant, so that the punishment
is meted out upon all the family.

There are a series of motifs in which barrenness, both human
reproductive and that of the land, are related to notions of
manhood, virility, the strength and seed of men and the way in
which male sexuality relates to political power. As Dorja travels,
trying to reconstruct himself after his castration, he dreams of
Genyen who appears as a spirit saying:

> I am still in that room, beyond the snow and the blocked passes. My
> real body . . . is locked in another room . . . I've just searched you
> out in my soul. I'm haunted by the thought you might hate me . . . I
> want your forgiveness.

In the dream she shows him a scarred back where her husband
whipped her until she confessed (she exposes herself onstage where
Dorja doesn't) to which Dorja replies: 'What are we men that we
can cause such pain?' Dorja has to re-define himself as a man:

> They said I'd never feel like this again. I can't do anything. I'm not
> a man. I can't feel like a man. That's the only way I can bear the
> weight . . . I want to enter you. To join you. Devil. You've worked
> your magic, go back to Jamyang. Let him laugh round the fire.
> You've brought me hell.

Then he 'rolls into a tight foetal ball'. His frustrated sexual desire
and his helplessness at the damage to him turns into fury at the
woman. Dorja demonstrates that desire can exist apart from
material reality. The imagination continues to work, whatever
happens to the body.

Dorja is taught meditation by a man called Kashog who promises
a form of revenge:

> But one night when you open your eyes she'll be standing there in
> front of you . . . in flesh and blood . . .

However, he realises that there is something about Dorja's desire
that he cannot identify. Dorja performs a ritual dance with a magic
dagger and a line of human forms appears behind him – members of
the Chinese People's Liberation Army. The imagination appears to
become political flesh, as the first Act ends.

In the second Act Dorja and the others are wearing Chinese

uniforms. They are all working, and much of the action demonstrates education and technology being brought to this relatively backward village. The monastery's land is seized and the monks starve. Tashi has to rely on the charity of others. The mother takes a central role when Tashi and Dorja argue, commenting maternally:

> The same over and over. You were bad enough as children . . . men. I'll have to do it all myself again.

Dorja is obsessed with revenge, his mother wants a quiet life:

> Why does the child never listen to his mother? We could have everything and you want to spit in their face.

It is as if the Tibetans are the demons of the Chinese, indicating that everyone has their particular dreams and visions as well as their demons.

Later Genyen is working a strip of land. Her husband Jamyang has died, and in spite of the fact that the Chinese have banned all religious ceremonies, she wants to bury him – an echo of Antigone. Dorja asks Tashi to say prayers (the Bardo) over Jamyang:

> TASHI: Why would you want to give the Bardo to your own worse enemy?
> DORJA: Perhaps because he is – was – my worst enemy. He understood nothing in this life. But in the end he prayed for someone to guide him back with a new understanding . . . There was still a desire there . . . Not to be born the same. Not to make the same mistakes. To grow.

Dorja respects the presence of desire, even in an enemy: 'Can we not turn our desires into reality?' As an act of spiritual and material generosity, he himself cuts Jamyang's body up with his butcher's knives, in keeping with the religious traditions of his people. Dorja has the final word:

> I work on the road, but I work like a donkey not like a man. My mind is full of dreams. I do not ask myself all the time who is this road for? Is it for the people . . . I should ask these questions more often, and out loud, so that my comrades can help me in answering them.

Dorja is a complicated phenomenon, someone who shows that desire, sexual and political, is always there. No social change can happen without desire and the imagination. Dorja's castration, the traditional act of 'unmanning', does nothing of the sort. His body is damaged, but his intellectual and social power are not. Sexuality and political power do not have to be synonymous, as the men in *Bad Apple* all believe. Dorja is a man who searches for personal identity as well as political meaning although sexuality is now denied him. Although the action follows his story, his family is an essential context, with the women fully represented as secondary characters.

Bent by Martin Sherman (Royal Court, 1979), begins in the living room of a gay couple in Berlin, 1934. Max and Rudi are having breakfast, Max having had a rather heavy night. Wolf, a naked blond man whom Max picked up, stumbles in. It is brittle, affectionate, semi-camp dialogue; Rudi comments:

> You called him your own little stormtrooper, you insulted all his friends. They left. I don't know why they didn't beat you up, but they didn't.

Two Nazis burst in, after the initial wit of the interior domestic scene, with full uniformed brutality.

Rudi and Max briefly hide out in Greta's club. Greta is a man in drag: 'Me? Everyone knows I'm not queer, I got a wife and kids.' Wolf turns out to have been the boyfriend of the stormtrooper's deputy in Berlin, but it is an irony that doesn't help Max. As Greta says: 'Now you're like Jews, unloved, baby, unloved.'

Max and Rudi leave, getting papers and tickets through the underground and hide out in a forest. They are found and put on a prisoner transport train where an officer tortures Rudi and finally kills him. To save his own life, Max doesn't interfere with the torture, and even allows himself to be forced into taking part.

Max is in a prison camp, with a yellow star, having said he is Jewish. He becomes friendly with another prisoner called Horst who wears a pink triangle, the symbol of a homosexual. Max says:

> I'm going to work a lot of deals . . . I'm only under protective custody, that's what they told me, I'm going to stay alive.

Max admits he is not Jewish, but he didn't want the pink star because it has the lowest connotations. He has no illusions about this: 'I'm a rotten person.'

Max continues to work deals. He and Horst break rocks, the two talking in a covert way. As they stand to attention on their brief rest period, there is an erotic exchange; Max says: 'We can't look at each other, we can't touch.' And Horst comments: 'We can feel . . . each other without looking, without touching.' The two make love through words, with desire and actuality related and separated, the taboo and the possible both being made explicit in one theatrical moment. Max understands the danger, warning Horst not to love him. When Horst is ill, Max gets medicine for him, even though he has to perform fellatio on the SS captain for it. Max comments on the irony that the captain thought that Max was Jewish:

Do you think that SS bastard would let a queer go down on him?

At the end Horst is killed, and Max touches him for the first time. He says he loved him, and puts on Horst's jacket with the pink triangle. Max is prepared now to take on his real identity and accept the consequences; he walks into the electric fence. The theme of homosexual persecution is highlighted because of the double nature of the taboo – both in 'normal' society and in the concentration camp, and the deeply personal act of sexuality is conveyed in the horrendously depersonalised context of the camp.

Many of the mixed cast plays of the 1970s were liberated into the world of political ideas, placing the individual (generally male) into his (sic) social setting. This appeared only possible by cutting off from the personal and the sexual, and by rejecting the domestic as anything more than one passing setting among many. With this, intra-familial relations and sexuality (through which the guts of interpersonal communication/conflict happen) are excluded. The intellectual passions of *Maydays* and *Occupations*, and the political statements of *Romans*, are of a different order intellectually, but not as emotionally engaging. The epic structures of these plays, spanning vast time-scales and using large casts, simply do not provide a depth of exploration for relationships between individual characters.

The association of women with the personal/emotional/sexual provides a further opportunity for imaginative displacement in the plays. By contrast, *Bad Apple* and *Bent*, without the imaginative distraction of women, present a broad range of relationships/ struggles between men in which male power, and subjective sexuality, are explored. In *Tibetan Inroads* male sexuality is its own reality and metaphor; there is no emotional or symbolic displacement onto the women, and there is a family with a mother at its centre; she may not develop politically, but she retains control of her emotional territory – the relationship with her sons.

Woman as Subject

Once a Catholic by Mary O'Malley
Piaf by Pam Gems
Steaming by Nell Dunn

The 1970s was also a decade which ended with successes for a small number of women playwrights. The first, *Once a Catholic* by Mary O'Malley (Royal Court, 1977) is set in a convent school somewhere in North London, and has a cast of ten women and four men. All the nuns have men's names – Mother Thomas Aquinas, Mother Peter, Mother Basil – and the girls are all called Mary, an ironic reminder of their virgin namesake. The play is set in 1956–7, the time of Jimmy Porter. While he was rebelling, the good Catholic girls of Willesden were being taught (hopefully) to become good wives and mothers. The scenes move between the convent school, the street and other locations.

In the chapel Father Mullarkey officiates and Mr Emanuelli plays the organ. In the classroom the nuns are in charge. One girl, Mary Mooney, is a fall-girl and everyone laughs at her. The girls are taught that:

> . . . every ordinary baby comes into the world with a stain upon its soul, the big black stain of original sin . . . and remember no sin ever goes unrecorded. Every little lapse will be brought to judgement.

Three girls who hate school discuss what they can do to get expelled, and one of them suggests:

> . . . you could make a big long willy out of plasticine and stick it on the crucifix in the chapel.

Mary Mooney is slow but has a beautiful voice and is tutored by Mr Emanuelli. She is also seriously religious, while her friends are more interested in boyfriends. In the biology lab Mother Basil dissects a female rabbit to give a lesson about the female reproductive organs. When Mary Mooney asks innocently how sperm gets into the vagina, she is thrown out of the classroom on the assumption that she is trying to embarrass the nun. The nuns assume 'such ignorance is inexcuseable in a girl of fifteen' but are not prepared to tell her the truth about sex. Their teaching denies passion, and preaches that sex is for marriage and reproduction. The other girls explain the facts of life to Mary Mooney, who still shares a bedroom with her parents. They talk about periods and contraceptives in a way that is observant, accurate and funny. Mooney puts her foot in it when she asks about the sin of sodomy.

Mary McGinty's boyfriend, Derek, accepts the double standard that sex before marriage is all right for boys but not for girls. Mary Gallagher's boyfriend, Cuthbert, is a spotty sixth-former, who drinks and smokes, and provides the information that the monks in the Middle Ages used to have lots of women. His talk about homosexuality includes prejudices about lesbians:

> It's easy to spot a lesbian, you know. They all have very short hair and big gruff voices.

In the following scene taboo-breaking is carried into the intimacy of the girls' lavatory where Mooney is reading in the Bible about menstruation and nakedness, until Mother Basil finds her.

Mary Mooney meets Derek and goes to his house where they snog. More taboo-breaking occurs when Mother Basil brings in a box of Tampax:

> No self-respecting girl would abuse her body with such a contraption, and that's a fact.

Mary McGinty with Derek, and Mary Gallagher with Cuthbert are planning their futures, which at least involve some degree of choice for them. Mary Mooney, who finds self-expression through singing, is advised by Emanuelli:

> You must learn to stand up for yourself or you'll find yourself trampled right into the ruddy ground. It will be better for you when you go away from this dump, this sanctimonious institution . . .

Emanuelli, with his gammy leg, is powerless in the convent – a damaged male in a women's community.

The final irony is played out movingly and painfully. Mary Mooney wants to sing for God and is the only one who wants to be a nun: 'I want to be as perfect as I possibly can and be sure of getting a high place in heaven.' When Mary McGinty sticks a long plastic penis on the crucifix in the chapel, the nuns assume it is Mary

Mooney, who is dragged in by the scruff of the neck, a scapegoat who can be punished for the sins of others, while they go free.

In Pam Gems' *Piaf* (Royal Shakespeare Company, 1978), the singer collapses during her first song, with the words: 'Get your fucking hands off me, I ain't done nothing yet.' We then flash back to the young Piaf, cold and singing in the streets, where again her first words to a man (the owner of a club) are: 'Get your fucking hands off me. . .' Piaf, whatever her situation, will not be patronised or told what to do.

The format of the play is simple: it chronicles Piaf's life, introducing her in a close friendship with Toine, who massages her feet:

Piaf . . . sits on the floor before Toine to have her hair done, an apparently loved and familiar ritual, to judge by her response.

Piaf climbs her way up the show business ladder. In a club when a man jeers at her, she responds: 'You've seen me drink – now you can watch me piss.' And she does so. This is followed by Piaf up against a wall 'getting it from a soldier', earning her money on the streets as best she may.

Piaf punctuates the action by singing, giving her the freedom to move between public performance and private life. One scene flows smoothly into another as she gets involved with the underworld and gradually becomes more and more successful. A man with whom she is involved advises her to keep the public and the private separate:

Your private life is your private life, Piaf, don't mix it . . . You don't have to stay in the gutter just because you were born there.

She and Toine talk about sex, showing a mixture of contempt for the opposite gender (when they can't perform as expected), with a dependence on them. Piaf is always shown as having a real resilience to the attempts of various men to exploit her. During the 1940s she helps the Resistance in Paris. The friendship with Toine continues, and although their fortunes occasionally diverge, it is a recurring base on which each of them can rely; Piaf still wants a man to make her happy:

. . . it's natural. I don't see why you should have to make excuses for it . . . I mean, the fact is I'm miserable on me own.

She meets Marcel, a boxer, and there is a scene in bed with

Marcel, cuddling and affectionate. Sexuality is something which consoles and comforts.

Piaf cannot separate the private and the public, the persona and the performance. The issue comes up in a conversation between Piaf and Marlene Dietrich:

PIAF: When I do a song, it's me that comes on. They get the lot.

MARLENE: Piaf, you can't have an orgasm every single time you walk on stage.

PIAF: I can.

Piaf's love of her audience is as great as her need to find a man she can love.

She passes from one lover to another, and after a bad car crash and becoming hooked on heroin, she ages, turning increasingly cynical about the glamour of show business:

They're after your balls, the lot of them . . . They all come looking for glamour . . . they all want a slice . . . Will they take the rough with the smooth? Will they hell. They want the bloody product – they want that all right, all wrapped up with feathers up its arse – but *songs*, they don't want SONGS! . . . My sort's dying out. Going extinct. What they want now is discs, they don't really want performance . . .

Even though Piaf's lifestyle is now that of the bourgeoisie, her language and emotional responses are still true to her origins. She sneers at Pierre, her former agent, for doing well:

You think being born working class is like having a disease.

Her final involvement is with Theo, a gentle young Greek boy who looks after her. In the last scene in the South of France with Theo, Toine is there to round out the structure of the play, so at the end Piaf has the three things that have been most important to her, a man, a good friend, and the memory of performance.

The final play, *Steaming* by Nell Dunn (Theatre Royal, Stratford, 1981) has an all-female cast: six women, all over thirty, and Bill 'a man who is heard but not seen'. The single set is the Turkish rest room of a 1909 public baths, in which, as in Maureen Duffy's play *Rites*, extremes of women's privacy are presented in a public place on women's territory. The baths are homely:

. . . to one side is a small table with some knitting and a radio on it and an armchair.

Violet, who manages the baths, has the kettle boiling and the radio on, functioning as a substitute mother-figure for the temporary home the baths provide for the women. There is no hot water, and in an argument between Violet and Bill, a contradictory dynamic is caught: the cosy comfort of a woman in control of her own territory, subject to a man's authority to make the structural hardware work. Gradually the women arrive. There is Josie, a bright, sparky woman obsessed with sex and her latest violent lover; Mrs Meadows and her daughter Dawn, who live in terrible slum conditions (Dawn appears to be retarded and is on pills; she only goes out once a week to come to the baths); and two middle class women, Nancy and Jane.

The women and the relationships, particularly those of Dawn and her mother, are poignantly presented. Dawn claims to have been raped by a policeman when she was sixteen. Mrs Meadows will not allow Dawn to take all her clothes off in the baths:

> . . . no, my Dawn's never even kissed me, we're not a kissing family.

The middle-class women are more mechanically written; Jane and her marriage, Nancy and her loneliness. The structural motif centres around whether or not the hot water is supplied, and as the scenes progress in the first Act, each set at weekly intervals, Violet begins to try to mend the pipes herself.

Much of the chat is about men – Josie discusses the men she gets involved with and from whom she can get more money than she can earn without qualifications, Jane and Nancy talk about past and present lovers and Mrs Meadows regrets the husband she no longer has. There is a contrast between Josie's pride and exhibitionism and Dawn's repression and fear of other people looking at her. In a fourth scene, Nancy, Jane and Violet have been inspecting the boiler and Vi threatens to complain to the town hall about the maintenance. Bill appears behind the glass door to give information about the pipes being corroded. At the end of the first Act Violet comes back to tell the other women the sudden news that in six weeks the baths are to be closed. Their haven is shattered.

In the second Act the solidarity between the women continues. On a personal level, they look after Mrs Meadows who is ill in bed in one of the cubicles, and in a more public way, Jane and Nancy plan to go to a meeting at the Town Hall to protest against the closure of the baths. During the course of this there is a brief moment of personal liberation when Josie gets Dawn to take all her clothes off and Dawn cavorts around in great pleasure at her new-found freedom, away from her mother's repression.

Towards the end, 'the shadow of Bill appears against the glass door', heralding the end of the play and Jane's comment to Nancy:

> Go for what you want, Nancy! We must put up a fight, even if we lose, we'll go down fighting.

This presages Josie, Vi and Dawn's return from the Town Hall to say they have lost. As Bill comes downstairs, Vi bolts the door and they decide to occupy the building. There is a utopian image as 'the stage goes misty as the women being to undress'. The final image is profoundly contradictory: a symbol of resistance and vulnerability from the women as they undress, of solidarity on a territory which is about to be taken from them.

These three plays with all-female casts, and women at the centre of the action, reveal new sets of preoccupations with the relationship between the public and the private, with specific reference to the experiences of women. The fluidity of setting in *Catholic* shifts between the convent (the institution in the control of the nuns and the Fathers) and the street or in the boys' houses. There are no scenes in any of the girls' family homes: their meetings are in school (beleaguered) or in the street (in transit). They have no territory of their own, and operate their small subversions on male-dominated territories. There are also no scenes between the nuns on their territory, and the relationship between nuns and pupils is simply that of the voice of bigoted, occasionally poignant, authority and those who are refusing to be led. The nuns are identified with the male hierarchy and power and are never allowed to be seen as female. This effectively defines the action in terms of the girls' tactics for personal survival rather than the gaining of real control; exploring sexual taboos onstage and the conflict between a repressive religious ideology and the burgeoning needs of young women. Mary Mooney is not merely a useful diversion for the other girls, but she also produces an interesting conflation between art and true faith, neither of which are appreciated by the nuns. Subjective devotion and self-expression are sub-themes to the dominant theme of female survival by minor tactics of subversion.

In *Piaf*, domestic scenes are resources for strength and support: friendship with Toine, love with the men. The ease and intimacy between the two women is absent from the girls' friendships in *Catholic*, and highlights what becomes imaginatively impossible when a female character is isolated from her own sex, and divided from others by hierarchy (Angelica/Polya and Maggie/Laura). Friendship, conflict, and the simple sharing of experience between women are simply not on the cards.

The taboos on the intimacies of female experience (the Tampax of *Catholic*) are taken a stage further in Piaf's use of crude language and the sexual and excretory acts she performs. Piaf has no biological family relationships, but Toine functions as a real, close, non-blood 'sister'.

In *Steaming* the territory is neutral, and momentarily collectively female (like *Rites* and *Catholic*). In the hermetic space the disparate group of women form an alternative family, complete with mother-figure, in which women acquire greater degrees of self-determination with support (and occasional conflict) from each other. Here, as in *Catholic* the structure of the female territory is determined by men, and the hermetic worlds of the women are the base camps from which support can be gained for whatever actual sexual and familial relationships the world may hold. The function of men is paradoxically supreme in terms of structural control, and relatively slight in terms of the internal dynamic of the plays, which are concerned with laying out some of the territory of female experience which lacks social power. Piaf, by contrast, has public power as a performer, and is seen also to have a meaningful (if fragmented) personal life. In her story the symbiotic relationship between public and private is demonstrated.

While these plays present women in groups, they also introduce woman as individual, not an atomised heroine at the centre of the play, or a metaphor for men's angst and conscience. Together with *Top Girls* they present women as a subject of drama and mistresses of their own destinies.

The Story So Far

Part Two

The second phase of post-war British drama opens with the end of censorship, and the influence of Brecht's play, *The Mother*, in which new ways of representing the nature of politics, women, and the public/private come into being. There is a world of difference between the contradictory messages of Brecht's play and the straightforward messages in *Saved*, *The Killing of Sister George* and *Staircase*. While the latter may not take on the important questions of socialist (or communist) revolution, their representation of women is more complex.

For Brecht, the Mother is a powerful figure: she is supposed to represent Mother Earth, the carer, the nurturer (perhaps even Mother Russia). In her 'realist' aspect she is presented as outside all productive relations, as the *tabula rasa* upon which is inscribed the journey of the most backward consciousness to the most progressive. Her femaleness is only useful insofar as its qualities can be harnessed to political activism outside the home. Once that has happened, the qualities themselves have no personal application, and the home itself is no longer relevant to the action, separating the female and the domestic from the political. The very notion of a varied representation of Woman, which includes the world of ideas and politics, is foreclosed; woman has become identified with all that is inimical to politics — unless, that is, she agrees to 'unsex' herself and join the boys. This is a very paradoxical political message for a theatrical era heralded by the liberation of plays from censorship.

The representation of sexuality is, however, much freer, with many playwrights taking advantage of the relaxation of censorship of language and what could be portrayed on stage: Arden (honesty of language), Duffy (the taboo set onstage, language), Williams (sex and the psyche), *Lay–By* (rape, pornography), Brenton (simulated homosexual rape), Sherman (homosexual love), O'Malley and Gems (breaking taboos for women) and Dunn (female nudity).

One of the most striking changes is that not one of the plays discussed has an exclusively domestic setting. More than that, only a very small number of the plays have even an occasional scene set in a character's home. This, too, has a contradictory significance. It represents a celebratory freeing of some parts of the theatrical imagination from the confines of the private home; it sets individuals in their different social and political contexts, and it frees women from their domestic role.

This results in a greater freedom in choice of setting, from the cosmos to the innermost recesses of the psyche, and also in the way that many playwrights move swiftly from location to location. Domestic scenes, when they occur, are used to make a narrative point rather than to explore the intertwining of place and personal relationships. The exceptions are the single–set plays by Dunn and Duffy, which occupy one public, neutral space, temporarily occupied by women; and the single set for *Occupations*, which is swept aside when characters make political speeches. Both ideologically and technically this new stage fluidity gave playwrights and directors a flexibility only thought possible in the high–tech media of radio, TV and film.

The family rarely appears in these plays, either in real or role–model terms: Griffiths has a kind of couple, but that relationship is over, and, in any case, is not explored in the world of the play, it is there for its shock and symbolic value; Brenton uses the family as a romantic reference point, Edgar nods tersely in its direction, and it doesn't appear at all in plays by O'Malley and Gems, Hare, Newman and Sherman. Unusually for this period, Churchill has a fierce scene between two sisters in *Top Girls*, and *Owners* is reminiscent of many plays of the Fifties and Sixties in that it seeks to portray the way ideas and social values impinge on inter–personal relationships. In content *Owners* harks back to the earlier decades, but in form it exploits the stage freedoms of the Seventies, without concentrating in great detail on specific relationships.

This abandonment of the domestic setting and its focus on the family, alters the representation of motherhood, women and politics. Motherhood is a role rather than a relationship for Arden, Duffy, O'Malley and Churchill, merits only a passing reference in plays by Gems, and is only one in a number of relationships portrayed by Dunn and Lowe.

While the mother may be largely dismissed from stage representation (real or symbolic) the sexual woman begins to appear more
explicitly; asserting her right to a self–chosen sexuality in plays by
Gems, Dunn, Churchill, Arden, Duffy and Williams; and
dangerous, to be destroyed, in *Lay–By* and plays by Hare. The
former approach is favoured largely by the female playwrights, the
latter by the males.

The political debate, source of much of the intellectual excitement in plays of this period, is staged in non–domestic settings but
there is still a gender dynamic which echoes that of the previous
decades. Although 'stories' based on the fortunes of individuals
have given way to 'histories' in the lives of groups of characters, the
gender divide is still clearly there. Only in all-female plays are
women the central subject, as in the plays of Arden, Duffy, Hare,
Churchill, O'Malley, Gems and Dunn, otherwise they are at the
service of the story, secondary, illustrative figures, rather than
symbolic. Thus, although the content of plays has broadened to
include any place, any time, any set of ideas, and the development
of different histories, women are not integrated into these various
possibilities. Again, paradoxically, this leaves women in mixed–cast
plays even more marginalised than they were in the earlier decades.
Women continue on occasion to be symbolically destroyed (Griffiths, Hare), or they take stage space for themselves in all–female
casts.

Above all, the dominant message is that the political is not the
personal. There are some exceptions to this: in *Tibetan Inroads*,
where Lowe explores the relationship between male sexuality,
power and ideals; in the all-male world of *Operation Bad Apple*,
where institutionalised relations are shown to be experienced profoundly at a subjective level; and in *Bent*, where the most cruel and
impersonal environment enables an intimate sexual relationship
between men. Over all, there is no exploration of heterosexual
relationships from either a male or female point of view.

Finally, with the plays forcefully taken outside the home, there is
no need for any particularly significant 'outsider' figure, such a
regular feature of plays from the Fifties and Sixties. Instead women
become the new outsiders to the representation of politics in a
larger world. They appear as subjects only on their own territory,
engaged with exploring its possibilities for survival, but not engaging at all with men at either the personal or political levels. In these

plays men are either absent or secondary characters.

On the whole, men are presented as custodians of public issues and political ideas, but, in keeping with the general tendencies of the plays of this period, are no longer concerned with the nature of masculinity, male sexuality or personal identity. The men inhabit the worlds of ideas and organisation, the women the world of survival.

Conclusion

We each begin probably with a little bias towards our own sex, and upon that bias build every circumstance in favour of it.

(Anne Elliot, in *Persuasion*, by Jane Austen.)

This concluding chapter must necessarily begin with a number of reminders and caveats. My general conclusions derive from a selected number of plays drawn from that part of theatre generally seen to be innovative and radical in form and content. These plays fall into the category of 'serious' or 'High' art – a category which raises all sorts of problematic questions. For the purposes of this book, the importance of it is that most of the plays have been taken as serious (though not necessarily un-comic) responses to contemporary society, and have achieved a fairly wide degree of popularity. It is by most of these plays that British drama of this period is known. I would not suggest at all that other kinds of plays – West End successes, for example – do not say important things about society. Merely that those are not the plays I've chosen to analyse here. My intention has been to suggest patterns of constancy, development and change during the two main phases of post-war British drama, which add up to an ideological picture of what were being expressed as the dominant world-views, through content, form and theatrical imagery.

In comparing these two theatrical landscapes I have chosen one or two plays by various playwrights, rather than following through the development of a much smaller number of individuals. This, too, has been deliberate, to see in what ways playwrights shared certain imaginative approaches, and in what ways they differed. The comments I have made throughout the book are about those particular plays, and not about the body of work by that particular playwright. Nor do the comments in any way represent judgements either on the playwright's intentions (since one can never fully know what they are) or on the playwright's personal views and beliefs. That is a fascinating and important exercise, but it is not one I have undertaken here.

This book began with two conceits: Virginia Woolf's Orlando, who begins life as a man, to be transformed halfway through into a woman; and my own speculations as to what would happen to the meanings in *Hamlet* were we to work on the assumption that the main character had undergone a sex/gender change and become a woman. Virginia Woolf implies that a change in gender will alter an individual's social future, in terms of the roles expected of them. My exercise with *Hamlet* aims to demonstrate that the aesthetic and social meanings generated by a dramatic text will vary according to the gender focus and bias of the work itself. This seems to me to be an obvious assumption which, once acknowledged, provides many exciting possibilities for the way we understand and interpret a play. To recognise that gender is an important variable in the creation of an imagined world, whatever its form, is to add richness to an understanding of the ways in which men and women imagine similarly and differently, in the same society, in relation to the same issues, or in relation to very different situations.

This has been my basic starting point. Closely related to that has been an interest in the way the family and sexuality have been represented in plays during and after theatre censorship. The figure of the mother has emerged as a key theme in the plays of the first period; in analysing the work of male and female playwrights, both similarities and differences have emerged. Also, because of the emphasis on the nature of the stage space – the 'setting' for plays – comparisons have been made between the relative balance of domestic/public settings, in relation to the above themes. And all these are drawn together in the ways playwrights have explored (or not) the connections or contradictions between interpersonal and institutional, or political relationships. Although working very much with the awareness that women are generally under-represented in theatre, my concern has been to analyse not just the way in which the female is represented, but what is characteristically significant about the ways in which the male is represented. Both men and women are gendered, after all. It is not a privilege or a handicap which belongs only to women, but a fact of social life everywhere which affects everyone.

Let me issue a final reminder about the critical importance of 1968, both because it heralded the end of theatre censorship, and therefore a fundamental change in the nature of the modern theatre industry, and also because it made possible an assimilation into theatre of all the exciting political and cultural ideas which had been building up throughout the 1960s. While I am aware that the 1950s and 1960s were not simply homogeneous decades, the fact remains that whatever the changes during this period, the overriding presence of theatre censorship provided a unifying framework. Similarly the 1970s and 1980s are not homogeneous – most of the plays discussed in this latter period fall in the 1970s, with some edging into the early 1980s. Certainly the 1970s were a decade of theatrical expansion, and much of that impetus has continued at least into the early 1980s. For the purposes, then, both of trying to deduce general patterns and of constructing an argument that I hope will be illuminating as well as provocative, here are my *general* conclusions based on the analysis of the plays in this book:

1950s/60s	1970s/80s

Gender dynamic

In mixed-cast plays by male playwrights, the action moves with the destinies of the male characters; in mixed-cast plays by women, the action moves with the destinies of the female characters; all-male cast plays tend to be written by men, all-female cast plays by women.

1950s/60s	1970s/80s
In plays by women, female characters in relation to men.	In plays by women, female characters in relation to each other.
In plays by men, male characters in relation to women.	In plays by men, male characters in relation to each other.

The family

1950s/60s	1970s/80s
Pervasive. Real, and as role model for other relationships, in plays by men and women.	Absent. People in groupings, in chosen social rather than biological relationships, in plays by men and women.

The Mother

1950s/60s	1970s/80s
Pervasive, though not always in control of the action in plays by men, generally more in control of the action in plays by women.	Entirely absent in any realistic form of relationship; figures occasionally as one social role among many in plays by and about women.

Look Back in Gender

<table>
<tr><td>1950s/60s</td><td>1970s/80s</td></tr>
</table>

Heterosexuality

Frequent, fraught and significant for male characters in plays by men.	Virtually absent, and never the central theme in plays by men.
Occasional and fraught in plays by women.	Mostly absent, and where present, fraught, treated with a mixture of dependence and contempt by characters in plays by women.

Homosexuality

Explicit in plays by men about men or women, sometimes sub-textual and homo-erotic, sometimes taboo and almost pornographic.	Either totally explicit as subject in plays by men about men, or totally absent. Lack of homo-erotic sub-text.
Absent in plays by and about women.	Absent in plays by and about women.

Male identity/manhood/masculinity

Pervasive in plays by men about men.	Absent in plays by men about men.
Occasionally explored in plays by women.	Absent in plays by women.

Female identity

Exploration of the place of woman in her familial/social world in plays by women about women.	More extensive exploration of women in their non-familial social roles, and as independent existential beings in plays by women about women.
Absent in plays by men.	Absent in plays by men.

Domestic settings

Very pervasive, many based round the single, domestic-set play by men and women. Stage fluidity only occasional.	Entirely absent as single-set, only cursorily included as an occasional scene in plays by both men and women. Stage fluidity a hallmark.
Men in control of the domestic space in plays by men.	

Conclusion

1950s/60s	1970s/80s

Public settings

Confined to occasional plays which are not based on a single domestic set, in plays by men and women.	Common both as realistic and polemic spaces in plays by men and women.

Representation of women

Powerfully symbolic of sexual and maternal power in plays by men, but not the subjects of the plays and not in control of the action. Partial outsiders.	Recognition of sexual power, dealt with by excluding women from main action, or symbolic annihilation, or as symbolic of romantic/heroic hope in plays by men. Outsiders.
As emerging subjects of the drama in plays by women, but mostly in relation to men.	Emphatic subjects of the drama in plays by women, in relation to other women, with strong references to the roles of men offstage.

Representation of men

In control of the action in both domestic and public worlds in plays by men.	In control of the action across history and politics in plays by men.
As fascinating, but often secondary characters in plays by women.	Either absent from the action, or as secondary characters, sometimes still structurally influencing the world and psyches of the female characters in plays by women.

Politics

Men bewildered, unsure, struggling to find causes and morality in plays by men.	Men in command, whatever the dilemmas. No deeply subjective questioning in plays by men.
Women actively engaged, sure of themselves in plays by men.	Women absent, except in the most token marginal way, symbolic of powerlessness, in plays by men.
Women engaged sometimes just with the domestic, sometimes also	Women seeking control over their life choices, not at all engaged

1950s/60s	1970s/80s
	Politics (continued)
with the political in plays by women.	with national/world politics or political ideas in plays by women.
Very little sense of links between politics and anything more than the immediate post-war period in plays by men and women. Low overt intellectual content. High emotional content.	Strong sense of politics as a part of the historical process, extending over long periods of time. High intellectual content, very low emotional content.
The political is incorporated with the personal in plays by men and women.	The political is violently separated from the personal in plays by men, and is not an issue in plays by women.

There are a number of observations to be made about these conclusions. The first – and probably the simplest – is that in both phases the dramatic action is impelled by one or other side of the gender divide. In the first phase more clearly according to whether it is the story of the male or female characters, in the second phase according to the way in which the span of history is seen through the eyes of the male or female characters. Almost without exception this derives from the gender bias of the author – according to whether the playwright is male or female, confirming the application of the quotation from Jane Austen at the beginning of this chapter.

From my point of view this has been the most expected conclusion, and one that should not be cause for regret, but rather for curiosity and interest. The gendered approach of a writer is reflected through the way her/his imagination focuses, not always in the same way, and not always predictably. This does not mean we have a ghettoised theatre in which men write 'well' about men and women write 'well' about women.

It means we have a theatre in which imaginations are always struggling to express new and different things, but in which gender is one of the most powerful constant filters, giving us profound insights into the way men see men and women see women, and indicating that leaping across the boundaries of the gendered imagination is still one of the major areas of development to be achieved. In theatre journalism during the 1970s plays by women were sometimes criticised for not 'developing' male characters fully enough. That criticism is itself mis-phrased. It is true in all plays that some characters are primary and some secondary; what this study has shown is that this divide works fairly consistently along gender lines. If we see it simply as the deficiency of the playwright, then we are talking about something negative; but if we see it as the positive vantage point from which the playwright views her/his world, then we are on the way to understanding why the world of the play takes the form it does.

The second observation concerns the differences between plays written before and after the repeal of the censorship laws. Certainly censorship did not keep playwrights away from the taboo – witness Osborne and Orton. Indeed, as a repressive measure, ever-present in the practical problems it threw up for the production of plays, it may have encouraged writers indirectly to explore the nature of repression in their plays. Relationships which challenge, subvert or violate conventional ideas about familial and sexual roles, appear continually in Phase One, as they do in Phase Two, accompanied by stronger language and more daring representations. The difference is that in Phase One they are placed in the context of personal struggle and in Phase Two they are simply accepted. This is because, as has already been pointed out, the family as a social unit has disappeared after 1968 in plays of this kind. Interestingly, the family appears even more intensely in plays by other playwrights, whose work has had West End success – for example, Alan Ayckbourn and Peter Nichols.

I would suggest that there is a cluster of reasons as to why the family has been so ruthlessly excluded (self-censored?) from the plays of Phase Two. Firstly, the influence of one of the most important Brechtian ideas, that the individual should be placed in his/her social and political context, has been actively and positively interpreted, but, as has been pointed out, also crudely and at the expense of the home and the family. Secondly, the influence of the feminist assertion that women's experiences are valid subject matter for drama, has enabled women playwrights to focus more consciously on writing about women, in many different ways. This has led women to explore what it is to be female outside of the family context – again, a positive and active development, which allows women the role of wife and mother at one remove from the central action of the play, but which leaves their familial roles unexplored. Thirdly, the definition of politics as outlined through the analysis, seems to need to demonstrate that political activism and personal life cannot go together, and must be ruthlessly separated. This implies also a separation between the intellect and the emotions, with men associated with organising the world and the intellect, and women as custodians of the emotions, separated from the world of the intellect and politics. The conclusion must be that far from demonstrating the slogan that 'the personal is political', Phase Two has again and again demonstrated (in plays by men *and* women) that the personal is the opposite of political, must be separated from it, and cannot be explored in relation to it. Sarah Kahn's deeply felt understanding of the way political conviction and personal life and relationships are absolutely inseparable is entirely absent from the apparently more politically self-conscious plays of the 1970s.

I have to admit that I am myself somewhat shocked and surprised by this conclusion. When I began work on this book, I did so with a particular personal take on the plays of both phases. My education in theatre had begun in the mid-1950s, when a particularly enlightened English teacher regularly booked us in to the Old Vic's five-year plan to stage all of Shakespeare; my brother took me to Stratford East to see the work of Joan Littlewood and Theatre Workshop and, when I went to Cambridge University in 1959, I plunged into the rich theatrical activity of the undergraduates, and acted in everything, from Miracle plays, Shakespeare and the Jacobeans, Restoration, to plays hot from the stage of the Royal Court Theatre, as well as work by European playwrights such as Brecht, Ionesco, Sartre.

In the 1970s I was equally intensely involved in the development of the new 'fringe' theatre; my plays were put on in pubs and some of the other impromptu theatre spaces which sprang up; I was also reviewing, and writing about, theatre, and engaged in many of the art/politics debates which took place so fiercely during that decade. In one sense I have always seen the plays from 1956 onwards as a continuum, with a watershed in the middle, but I did wonder, as I embarked on this book, whether I would find the Phase One plays politically naive and Phase Two plays politically sophisticated; I wondered also what I might find had changed in the way men and women had been represented in the two phases, and I was fairly sure that I would see the development from Phase One to Two as a simple linear progression forwards in all respects.

Conclusion

The reality, however, is more complex than this. It is not merely a matter of coming out of official censorship into a clearing of public plays full of great freedom of expression. It is more a question of two steps forward in one direction and one step backwards in another. It could be claimed that from writing under the shadow of official censorship, and trying to find oblique, imaginative ways of expressing sexual and political taboos, playwrights moved into writing under the shadow of a self-censorship, which separated the sexual from the political, and has claimed the family as a new implicit taboo.

Feminist and socialist critiques of the oppressive aspects of the family, particularly in relation to gender roles, account for this to some extent, but the reality of lives lived in families – for playwrights as well as the majority of the population – and if not in families, then in interpersonal/sexual relations of various kinds – is still a material reality in post-1968 society. The post-1968 plays virtually ignore this. Perhaps this new taboo is in part also linked to the educational and political differences which produced a generation of largely university-educated playwrights in post-1968, whose formal education was supplemented by either being involved in, or certainly aware of, the intellectual and political debates of great sophistication which engaged the intellectuals of the new left which led them to place more value on the intellectual than the emotional.

Combine this with an over-simple interpretation of Brecht, a heady desire to exploit the new freedoms of the stage, the sub-conscious imaginative associations between women/emotions/home, and a new split appears between politics and the personal, the intellect and the emotions, and men and women. Women playwrights write about women relating to other women, men playwrights write about men relating to men, both revealing powerful gender-dynamics. But neither men nor women explore the inter-relationship between men and women, or the private and the public, despite feminism's insistence on this as a critical step in understanding how society works and how people live their lives.

While we can look back to the 1970s and find plays which bring the whole of history onto the stage, which encompass social satire, intellectual insight into the workings of political parties and groups, the power dynamics of male-dominated institutions, and a new representation of women as existential subject matter, we have to look back to the 1950s and 60s for insights into the way the family functions under stress, the way individuals struggle to define personal identity in relation to social and political conviction, and for a representation of women which, while it may be loaded with some of the prejudices of male-bias, exerts a powerful theatrical symbolism which acknowledges the importance of the figure of the mother and of women as sexual beings, in plays by men and women.

Perhaps an ideal prognosis for the future would be a school of playwrighting which combined the strengths of both phases: a theatre which did not abandon the domestic in favour of the public, but sought to explore the relationship between the two. A theatre which acknowledged its male/female gender biases, but also sought to explore the relationship between the two instead of ignoring it. A theatre which celebrated its intellectual strengths without abandoning the murky risks of stage imagery; and in which this imagery utilised male figures as well as female figures; a theatre certainly in which there were as many women as men writing, so that the stage-world views were genuinely expanded and enriched. Above all, a theatre in which no one felt that they were constrained as prisoners of gender, but rather that the gendered approach which we all have was recognised as a source of great strength. Such a theatre is probably truly an ideal, but then, in the world of the imagination, anything is possible.

Select Bibliography of Plays

The arrangement follows the order of the chapters in the book. The only plays listed are those mentioned in the chapter headings or quoted in the text. The dates refer to editions which have been quoted.

William Shakespeare *Hamlet*: Penguin, 1958
John Osborne *Look Back in Anger*; *A Patriot for Me*: Faber, 1978 and 1971
Arnold Wesker *Chicken Soup with Barley*; *Roots*; *I'm Talking About Jerusalem*: Penguin, 1975
Samuel Beckett *Waiting for Godot*: Faber, 1959
Harold Pinter *The Room*; *The Birthday Party*: Methuen, 1976
John Arden *Serjeant Musgrave's Dance*: Methuen, 1960
Shelagh Delaney *A Taste of Honey*: Methuen, 1975
Ann Jellicoe *The Sport of My Mad Mother*; *The Knack*: Faber, 1964 and 1969
Doris Lessing *Each His Own Wilderness*: Penguin, 1959; *Play With a Tiger*: Davis-Poynter, 1972
Joe Orton *Entertaining Mr Sloane*; *Loot*: Methuen, 1973 and 1976
Edward Bond *Saved*: Methuen, 1977
Frank Marcus *The Killing of Sister George*: Samuel French, 1965
Charles Dyer *Staircase*: Samuel French, 1966
Bertolt Brecht *The Mother*: Methuen, 1978
Jane Arden *Vagina Rex and the Gas Oven*: Calder & Boyars, 1971
Maureen Duffy *Rites*: Vintage, 1974
Heathcote Williams *AC/DC*: John Calder, 1982
Howard Brenton, Brian Clark, Trevor Griffiths, David Hare, Stephen Poliakoff, Hugh Stoddart, Snoo Wilson *Lay-By*: Calder & Boyars, 1972
Trevor Griffiths *Occupations*: Faber, 1980
David Hare *Slag*; *Teeth 'n' Smiles*: Faber, 1971 and 1976
Howard Brenton *The Romans in Britain*: Methuen, 1980

Select Bibliography of Plays

Caryl Churchill *Owners*; *Top Girls*: Methuen, 1973 and 1984
David Edgar *Destiny*; *Maydays*: Methuen, 1976 and 1983
G F Newman *Operation Bad Apple*: Methuen, 1982
Stephen Lowe *Tibetan Inroads*: Methuen/Royal Court, 1981
Martin Sherman *Bent*: Avon Books, 1979
Mary O'Malley *Once a Catholic*: Amber Lane Press, 1978
Pam Gems *Piaf*: Amber Lane Press, 1979
Nell Dunn *Steaming*: Amber Lane Press, 1982

Index

Index